In the name of God, the Gracious, the Merciful. By Time. The human being is in loss. Except those who believe, and do good works, and encourage truth, and recommend patience.

Time

ISLAM

Through Quran

Selection of Quran Chapters

TRANSLATED BY TALAL ITANI

ISLAM

Through Quran

Translated from Arabic by Talal Itani

Published by ClearQuran
Dallas • Beirut

Copyright © 2015 ClearQuran

www.ClearQuran.com

Chapters (Suras)

The Opening ....(al-Fatihah)................................ 1
The Heifer ....(al-Baqarah) 1
Family of Imran ....(Ali 'Imran)................................ 28
Joseph ....(Yusuf) 43
Abraham ....(Ibrahim) 52
The Bee ....(an-Nahl).................................. 56
The Night Journey ......(al-Isra') 65
Mary ....(Maryam) 72
Ta-Ha ....(Ta-Ha)..................................... 78
The Pilgrimage ....(al-Hajj) 86
The Poets ....(ash-Shu'ara') 92
History ....(al-Qasas) 100
Luqman ....(Luqman)................................ 107
Prostration ....(as-Sajdah) 110
Originator ....(Fatir) 112
Ya-Seen ....(Ya-Seen) 115
Throngs ....(az-Zumar) 120
Detailed ....(Fussilat) 125
Kneeling ....(al-Jathiyah) 129
The Dunes ....(al-Ahqaf)................................ 132
Muhammad ....(Muhammad)........................... 135
Victory ....(al-Fath)................................... 138
Qaf ....(Qaf).. 140
The Compassionate ...(ar-Rahman) 143
The Inevitable ....(al-Waqi'ah) 145

Iron	(al-Hadid`)	149
Column	(as-Saff)	152
Gathering	(at-Taghabun)	153
The Enwrapped	(al-Muzzammil)	154
The Enrobed	(al-Muddathir)	155
Resurrection	(al-Qiyamah)	157
The Event	(an-Naba')	159
The Rolling	(at-Takwir)	160
The Shattering	(al-Infitar)	161
The Defrauders	(al-Mutaffifin)	162
The Rupture	(al-Inshiqaq)	164
The Constellations	(al-Buruj)	165
The Most High	(al-A'la)	166
The Overwhelming	(al-Ghashiyah)	166
The Dawn	(al-Fajr)	167
The Land	(al-Balad)	168
The Night	(al-Layl)	169
Morning Light	(adh-Duha)	170
The Soothing	(ash-Sharh)	171
The Fig	(at-Tin)	171
Decree	(al-Qadr)	171
The Quake	(az-Zalzalah)	172
Time	(al-'Asr)	172
The Backbiter	(al-Humazah)	172
The Disbelievers	(al-Kafirun)	173
Monotheism	(al-Ikhlas)	173

The Opening (al-Fatihah)

1 In the name of God, the Gracious, the Merciful.

2 Praise be to God, Lord of the Worlds.

3 The Most Gracious, the Most Merciful.

4 Master of the Day of Judgment.

5 It is You we worship, and upon You we call for help.

6 Guide us to the straight path.

7 The path of those You have blessed, not of those against whom there is anger, nor of those who are misguided.

The Heifer (al-Baqarah)

In the name of God, the Gracious, the Merciful.

1 Alif, Lam, Meem.

2 This is the Book in which there is no doubt, a guide for the righteous.

3 Those who believe in the unseen, and perform the prayers, and give from what We have provided for them.

4 And those who believe in what was revealed to you, and in what was revealed before you, and are certain of the Hereafter.

5 These are upon guidance from their Lord. These are the successful.

6 As for those who disbelieve—it is the same for them, whether you have warned them, or have not warned them—they do not believe.

7 God has set a seal on their hearts and on their hearing, and over their vision is a veil. They will have a severe torment.

8 Among the people are those who say, "We believe in God and in the Last Day," but they are not believers.

9 They seek to deceive God and those who believe, but they deceive none but themselves, though they are not aware.

10 In their hearts is sickness, and God has increased their sickness. They will have a painful punishment because of their denial.

11 And when it is said to them, "Do not make trouble on earth," they say, "We are only reformers."

12 In fact, they are the troublemakers, but they are not aware.

13 And when it is said to them, "Believe as the people have believed," they say, "Shall we believe as the fools have believed?" In fact, it is they who are the fools, but they do not know.

14 And when they come across those who believe, they say, "We believe"; but when they are alone with their devils, they say, "We are with you; we were only ridiculing."

15 It is God who ridicules them, and leaves them bewildered in their transgression.

16 Those are they who have bartered error for guidance; but their trade does not profit them, and they are not guided.

17 Their likeness is that of a person who kindled a fire; when it illuminated all around him, God took away their light, and left them in darkness, unable to see.

18 Deaf, dumb, blind. They will not return.

19 Or like a cloudburst from the sky, in which is darkness, and thunder, and lightning. They press their fingers into their ears from the thunderbolts, in fear of death. But God surrounds the disbelievers.

20 The lightning almost snatches their sight away. Whenever it illuminates for them, they walk in it; but when it grows dark over them, they stand still. Had God willed, He could have taken away their hearing and their sight. God is capable of everything.

21 O people! Worship your Lord who created you and those before you, that you may attain piety.

22 He who made the earth a habitat for you, and the sky a structure, and sends water down from the sky, and brings out fruits thereby, as a sustenance for you. Therefore, do not assign rivals to God while you know.

23 And if you are in doubt about what We have revealed to Our servant, then produce a chapter like these, and call your witnesses apart from God, if you are truthful.

24 But if you do not—and you will not—then beware the Fire whose fuel is people and stones, prepared for the disbelievers.

25 And give good news to those who believe and do righteous deeds; that they will have gardens beneath which rivers flow. Whenever they are provided with fruit therefrom as sustenance, they will say, "This is what we were provided with before," and they will be given the like of it. And they will have pure spouses therein, and they will abide therein forever.

26 God does not shy away from making an example of a gnat, or something above it. As for those who believe, they know that it is the Truth from their Lord. But as for those who disbelieve, they say, "What did God intend by this example?" He leads astray many thereby, and He guides many thereby; but He misleads thereby only the evildoers.

27 Those who violate God's covenant after its confirmation, and sever what God has commanded to be joined, and commit evil on earth. These are the losers.

28 How can you deny God, when you were dead and He gave you life, then He will put you to death, then He will bring you to life, then to Him you will be returned?

29 It is He who created for you everything on earth, then turned to the heaven, and made them seven heavens. And He is aware of all things.

30 When your Lord said to the angels, "I am placing a successor on earth." They said, "Will You place in it someone who will cause corruption in it and shed blood, while we declare Your praises and sanctify You?" He said, "I know what you do not know."

31 And He taught Adam the names, all of them; then he presented them to the angels, and said, "Tell Me the names of these, if you are sincere."

32 They said, "Glory be to You! We have no knowledge except what You have taught us. It is you who are the Knowledgeable, the Wise."

33 He said, "O Adam, tell them their names." And when he told them their names, He said, "Did I not tell you that I know the secrets of the heavens and the earth, and that I know what you reveal and what you conceal?"

34 And We said to the angels, "Bow down to Adam." They bowed down, except for Satan. He refused, was arrogant, and was one of the disbelievers.

35 We said, "O Adam, inhabit the Garden, you and your spouse, and eat from it freely as you please, but do not approach this tree, lest you become wrongdoers."

36 But Satan caused them to slip from it, and caused them to depart the state they were in. We said, "Go down, some of you enemies of one another. And you will have residence on earth, and enjoyment for a while."

37 Then Adam received words from his Lord, so He relented towards him. He is the Relenting, the Merciful.

38 We said, "Go down from it, all of you. Yet whenever guidance comes to you from Me, then whoever follows My guidance—they have nothing to fear, nor shall they grieve.

39 But as for those who disbelieve and reject Our signs—these are the inmates of the Fire—wherein they will remain forever."

40 O Children of Israel! Remember My blessings which I bestowed upon you, and fulfill your pledge to Me, and I will fulfill My pledge to you, and fear Me.

41 And believe in what I revealed, confirming what is with you; and do not be the first to deny it; and do not exchange My revelations for a small price; and be conscious of Me.

42 And do not mix truth with falsehood, and do not conceal the truth while you know.

43 And attend to your prayers, and practice regular charity, and kneel with those who kneel.

44 Do you command people to virtuous conduct, and forget yourselves, even though you read the Scripture? Do you not understand?

45 And seek help through patience and prayer. But it is difficult, except for the devout.

46 Those who know that they will meet their Lord, and that to Him they will return.

47 O Children of Israel! Remember My favor which I bestowed upon you, and I that favored you over all nations.

48 And beware of a Day when no soul will avail another in the least, nor will any intercession be accepted on its behalf, nor will any ransom be taken from it, nor will they be helped.

49 And recall that We delivered you from the people of Pharaoh. They inflicted on you terrible persecution, killing your sons and sparing your women. Therein was a tremendous trial from your Lord.

50 And recall that We parted the sea for you, so We saved you, and We drowned the people of Pharaoh as you looked on.

51 And recall that We appointed for Moses forty nights. Then you took to worshiping the calf after him, and you turned wicked.

52 Then We pardoned you after that, so that you might be grateful.

53 And recall that We gave Moses the Scripture and the Criterion, so that you may be guided.

54 And recall that Moses said to his people, "O my people, you have done wrong to yourselves by worshiping the calf. So repent to your Maker, and kill your egos. That would be better for you with your Maker." So He turned to you in repentance. He is the Accepter of Repentance, the Merciful.

55 And recall that you said, "O Moses, we will not believe in you unless we see God plainly." Thereupon the thunderbolt struck you, as you looked on.

56 Then We revived you after your death, so that you may be appreciative.

57 And We shaded you with clouds, and We sent down to you manna and quails: "Eat of the good things We have provided for you." They did not wrong Us, but they used to wrong their own souls.

58 And recall that We said, "Enter this town, and eat plentifully from it whatever you wish; but enter the gate humbly, and say, 'Pardon.' We will forgive your sins, and give increase to the virtuous."

59 But the wrongdoers among them substituted words other than those given to them, so We sent down on the wrongdoers a plague from heaven, because of their wicked behavior.

60 And recall when Moses prayed for water for his people. We said, "Strike the rock with your staff." Thereupon twelve springs gushed out from it, and each tribe recognized its drinking-place. "Eat and drink from God's provision, and do not corrupt the earth with disobedience."

61 And recall when you said, "O Moses, we cannot endure one kind of food, so call to your Lord to produce for us of what the earth grows: of its herbs, and its cucumbers, and its garlic, and its lentils, and its onions." He said, "Would you substitute worse for better? Go down to Egypt, where you will have what you asked for." They were struck with humiliation and poverty, and incurred wrath from God. That was because they rejected God's revelations and wrongfully killed the prophets. That was because they disobeyed and transgressed.

62 Those who believe, and those who are Jewish, and the Christians, and the Sabeans—any who believe in God and the Last Day, and act righteously—will have their reward with their Lord; they have nothing to fear, nor will they grieve.

63 And recall when We received a pledge from you, and raised the Mount above you: "Take what We have given you earnestly, and remember what is in it, that you may attain righteousness."

64 But after that you turned away. Were it not for God's grace and mercy towards you, you would have been among the losers.

65 And you surely knew those of you who violated the Sabbath. We said to them, "Be despicable apes!"

66 Thus We made it a deterrent for their generation, and for subsequent generations, and a lesson for the righteous.

67 And recall when Moses said to his people, "God commands you to sacrifice a heifer." They said, "Do you make a mockery of us?" He said, "God forbid that I should be so ignorant."

68 They said, "Call upon your Lord to show us which one." He said, "He says she is a heifer, neither too old, nor too young, but in between. So do what you are commanded."

69 They said, "Call upon your Lord to show us what her color is." He said, "He says she is a yellow heifer, bright in color, pleasing to the beholders."

70 They said, "Call upon your Lord to show us which one; the heifers look alike to us; and God willing, we will be guided."

71 He said, "He says she is a heifer, neither yoked to plow the earth, nor to irrigate the field; sound without blemish." They said, "Now you have brought the truth." So they slew her; though they almost did not.

72 And recall when you killed a person, and disputed in the matter; but God was to expose what you were hiding.

73 We said, "Strike him with part of it." Thus God brings the dead to life; and He shows you His signs, that you may understand.

74 Then after that your hearts hardened. They were as rocks, or even harder. For there are some rocks from which rivers gush out, and others that splinter and water comes out from them, and others that sink in awe of God. God is not unaware of what you do.

75 Do you hope that they will believe in you, when some of them used to hear the Word of God, and then deliberately distort it, even after understanding it?

76 And when they come across those who believe, they say, "We believe," but when they come together privately, they say, "Will you inform them of what

God has disclosed to you, so that they might dispute with you concerning it before your Lord?" Do you not understand?

77 Do they not know that God knows what they conceal and what they reveal?

78 And among them are uneducated who know the Scripture only through hearsay, and they only speculate.

79 So woe to those who write the Scripture with their own hands, and then say, "This is from God," that they may exchange it for a little price. Woe to them for what their hands have written, and woe to them for what they earn.

80 And they say, "The Fire will not touch us except for a number of days." Say, "Have you received a promise from God—God never breaks His promise—or are you saying about God what you do not know?"

81 Indeed, whoever commits misdeeds, and becomes besieged by his iniquities—these are the inmates of the Fire, wherein they will dwell forever.

82 As for those who believe and do righteous deeds—these are the inhabitants of Paradise, wherein they will dwell forever.

83 We made a covenant with the Children of Israel: "Worship none but God; and be good to parents, and relatives, and orphans, and the needy; and speak nicely to people; and pray regularly, and give alms." Then you turned away, except for a few of you, recanting.

84 And We made a covenant with you: "You shall not shed the blood of your own, nor shall you evict your own from your homes." You agreed, and were all witnesses.

85 But here you are, killing your own, and expelling a group of your own from their homes—conspiring against them in wrongdoing and hostility. And if they come to you as captives, you ransom them, although it was forbidden to you. Is it that you believe in part of the Scripture, and disbelieve in part? What is the reward for those among you who do that but humiliation in this life? And on the Day of Resurrection, they will be assigned to the most severe torment. God is not unaware of what you do.

86 Those are they who bought the present life for the Hereafter, so the punishment will not be lightened for them, nor will they be helped.

87 We gave Moses the Scripture, and sent a succession of messengers after him. And We gave Jesus son of Mary the clear proofs, and We supported him with the Holy Spirit. Is it that whenever a messenger comes to you with anything

your souls do not desire, you grew arrogant, calling some impostors, and killing others?

88 And they said, "Our hearts are sealed." Rather, God has cursed them for their ingratitude. They have little faith.

89 And when a scripture came to them from God, confirming what they have—although previously they were seeking victory against those who disbelieved—but when there came to them what they recognized, they disbelieved in it. So God's curse is upon the disbelievers.

90 Miserable is what they sold their souls for—rejecting what God has revealed, out of resentment that God would send down His grace upon whomever He chooses from among His servants. Thus they incurred wrath upon wrath. And there is a demeaning punishment for the disbelievers.

91 And when it is said to them, "Believe in what God has revealed," they say, "We believe in what was revealed to us," and they reject anything beyond that, although it is the truth which confirms what they have. Say, "Why did you kill God's prophets before, if you were believers?"

92 Moses came to you with clear proofs, yet you adopted the calf in his absence, and you were in the wrong.

93 And We made a covenant with you, and raised the Mount above you: "Take what We have given you firmly, and listen." They said, "We hear and disobey." And their hearts became filled with the love of the calf because of their disbelief. Say, "Wretched is what your faith commands you to do, if you are believers."

94 Say, "If the Final Home with God is yours alone, to the exclusion of all other people, then wish for death if you are sincere."

95 But they will never wish for it, because of what their hands have forwarded. God is aware of the evildoers.

96 You will find them, of all mankind, the most eager for life, even more than the polytheists. Every one of them wishes he could live a thousand years; but to be granted a long life will not nudge him from the punishment. God is Seeing of what they do.

97 Say, "Whoever is hostile to Gabriel—it is he who revealed it to your heart by God's leave, confirming what preceded it, and guidance and good news for the believers."

98 Whoever is hostile to God, and His angels, and His messengers, and Gabriel, and Michael—God is hostile to the faithless.

99 We have revealed to you clear signs, and none rejects them except the sinners.

100 Is it not that whenever they make a covenant, some of them toss it aside? In fact, most of them do not believe.

101 And when there came to them a messenger from God, confirming what they had, a faction of those who were given the Book threw the Book of God behind their backs, as if they do not know.

102 And they followed what the devils taught during the reign of Solomon. It was not Solomon who disbelieved, but it was the devils who disbelieved. They taught the people witchcraft and what was revealed in Babylon to the two angels Harut and Marut. They did not teach anybody until they had said, "We are a test, so do not lose faith." But they learned from them the means to cause separation between man and his wife. But they cannot harm anyone except with God's permission. And they learned what would harm them and not benefit them. Yet they knew that whoever deals in it will have no share in the Hereafter. Miserable is what they sold their souls for, if they only knew.

103 Had they believed and been righteous, the reward from God would have been better, if they only knew.

104 O you who believe! Do not say ambiguous words, but say words of respect, and listen. The disbelievers will have a painful torment.

105 It is never the wish of the disbelievers from among the People of the Book, nor of the polytheists, that any good should be sent down to you from your Lord. But God chooses for His mercy whomever He wills. God is Possessor of Sublime Grace.

106 We never nullify a verse, nor cause it to be forgotten, unless We bring one better than it, or similar to it. Do you not know that God is capable of all things?

107 Do you not know that to God belongs the sovereignty of the heavens and the earth, and that apart from God you have no guardian or helper?

108 Or do you want to question your Messenger as Moses was questioned before? Whoever exchanges faith for disbelief has strayed from the right path.

109 Many of the People of the Book wish to turn you back into unbelievers after you have believed, out of envy on their part, after the Truth has become clear to them. But pardon and overlook, until God brings His command. God has power over all things.

110 And perform the prayer, and give alms. Whatever good you forward for yourselves, you will find it with God. God is Seeing of everything you do.

111 And they say, "None will enter Heaven unless he is a Jew or a Christian." These are their wishes. Say, "Produce your proof, if you are truthful."

112 In fact, whoever submits himself to God, and is a doer of good, will have his reward with his Lord—they have nothing to fear, nor shall they grieve.

113 The Jews say, "The Christians are not based on anything;" and the Christians say, "The Jews are not based on anything." Yet they both read the Scripture. Similarly, the ignorant said the same thing. God will judge between them on the Day of Resurrection regarding their differences.

114 Who is more unjust than him who forbids the remembrance of God's name in places of worship, and contributes to their ruin? These ought not to enter them except in fear. For them is disgrace in this world, and for them is a terrible punishment in the Hereafter.

115 To God belong the East and the West. Whichever way you turn, there is God's presence. God is Omnipresent and Omniscient.

116 And they say, "God has begotten a son." Be He glorified. Rather, His is everything in the heavens and the earth; all are obedient to Him.

117 Originator of the heavens and the earth. Whenever He decrees a thing, He says to it, "Be," and it becomes.

118 Those who do not know say, "If only God would speak to us, or a sign would come to us." Thus said those who were before them. Their hearts are alike. We have made the signs clear for people who are certain.

119 We have sent you with the truth—bringing good news, and giving warnings. You will not be questioned about the inmates of Hell.

120 The Jews and the Christians will not approve of you, unless you follow their creed. Say, "God's guidance is the guidance." Should you follow their desires, after the knowledge that has come to you, you will have in God neither guardian nor helper.

121 Those to whom We have given the Scripture follow it, as it ought to be followed—these believe in it. But as for those who reject it—these are the losers.

122 O Children of Israel! Remember My blessing which I bestowed upon you, and that I have favored you over all people.

123 And beware of a Day when no soul will avail another soul in any way, and no ransom will be accepted from it, and no intercession will benefit it, and they will not be helped.

124 And when his Lord tested Abraham with certain words, and he fulfilled them. He said, "I am making you a leader of humanity." He said, "And my descendants?" He said, "My pledge does not include the wrongdoers."

125 And We made the House a focal point for the people, and a sanctuary. Use the shrine of Abraham as a place of prayer. And We commissioned Abraham and Ishmael, "Sanctify My House for those who circle around it, and those who seclude themselves in it, and those who kneel and prostrate."

126 When Abraham said, "O My Lord, make this a peaceful land, and provide its people with fruits—whoever of them believes in God and the Last Day." He said, "And whoever disbelieves, I will give him a little enjoyment, then I will consign him to the punishment of the Fire; how miserable the destiny!"

127 As Abraham raises the foundations of the House, together with Ishmael, "Our Lord, accept it from us, You are the Hearer, the Knower.

128 Our Lord, and make us submissive to You, and from our descendants a community submissive to You. And show us our rites, and accept our repentance. You are the Acceptor of Repentance, the Merciful.

129 Our Lord, and raise up among them a messenger, of themselves, who will recite to them Your revelations, and teach them the Book and wisdom, and purify them. You are the Almighty, the Wise."

130 Who would forsake the religion of Abraham, except he who fools himself? We chose him in this world, and in the Hereafter he will be among the righteous.

131 When his Lord said to him, "Submit!" He said, "I have submitted to the Lord of the Worlds."

132 And Abraham exhorted his sons, and Jacob, "O my sons, God has chosen this religion for you, so do not die unless you have submitted."

133 Or were you witnesses when death approached Jacob, and he said to his sons, "What will you worship after Me?" They said, "We will worship your God, and the God of your fathers, Abraham, Ishmael, and Isaac; One God; and to Him we submit."

134 That was a community that has passed; for them is what they have earned, and for you is what you have earned; and you will not be questioned about what they used to do.

135 And they say, "Be Jews or Christians, and you will be guided." Say, "Rather, the religion of Abraham, the Monotheist; he was not an idolater."

136 Say, "We believe in God; and in what was revealed to us; and in what was revealed to Abraham, and Ishmael, and Isaac, and Jacob, and the Patriarchs; and in what was given to Moses and Jesus; and in what was given to the prophets—from their Lord. We make no distinction between any of them, and to Him we surrender."

137 If they believe in the same as you have believed in, then they have been guided. But if they turn away, then they are in schism. God will protect you against them; for He is the Hearer, the Knower.

138 God's coloring. And who gives better coloring than God? "And we are devoted to Him."

139 Say, "Do you argue with us about God, when He is our Lord and your Lord, and We have our works, and you have your works, and we are sincere to Him?"

140 Or do you say that Abraham, Ishmael, Isaac, Jacob, and the Patriarchs were Jews or Christians? Say, "Do you know better, or God?" And who does greater wrong than he who conceals a testimony he has from God? God is not unaware of what you do.

141 That was a community that has passed. To them is what they have earned, and to you is what you have earned. And you will not be questioned about what they used to do.

142 The ignorant among the people will say, "What has turned them away from the direction of prayer they once followed?" Say, "To God belong the East and the West. He guides whom He wills to a straight path."

143 Thus We made you a moderate community, that you may be witnesses to humanity, and that the Messenger may be a witness to you. We only established the direction of prayer, which you once followed, that We may distinguish those who follow the Messenger from those who turn on their heels. It is indeed difficult, except for those whom God has guided. But God would never let your faith go to waste. God is Kind towards the people, Merciful.

144 We have seen your face turned towards the heaven. So We will turn you towards a direction that will satisfy you. So turn your face towards the Sacred

Mosque. And wherever you may be, turn your faces towards it. Those who were given the Book know that it is the Truth from their Lord; and God is not unaware of what they do.

145 Even if you were to bring to those who were given the Book every proof, they would not follow your direction, nor are you to follow their direction, nor do they follow the direction of one another. And if you were to follow their desires, after the knowledge that has come to you, you would be in that case one of the wrongdoers.

146 Those to whom We have given the Book recognize it as they recognize their own children. But some of them conceal the truth while they know.

147 The truth is from your Lord, so do not be a skeptic.

148 To every community is a direction towards which it turns. Therefore, race towards goodness. Wherever you may be, God will bring you all together. God is capable of everything.

149 And wherever you come from, turn your face towards the Sacred Mosque. This is the truth from your Lord, and God is not heedless of what you do.

150 And wherever you come from, turn your face towards the Sacred Mosque. And wherever you may be, turn your faces towards it. So that the people may not have any argument against you—except those who do wrong among them. So do not fear them, but fear Me, that I may complete My blessings upon you, and that you may be guided.

151 Just as We sent to you a messenger from among you, who recites Our revelations to you, and purifies you, and teaches you the Book and wisdom, and teaches you what you did not know.

152 So remember Me, and I will remember you. And thank Me, and do not be ungrateful.

153 O you who believe! Seek help through patience and prayers. God is with the steadfast.

154 And do not say of those who are killed in the cause of God, "Dead." Rather, they are alive, but you do not perceive.

155 We will certainly test you with some fear and hunger, and some loss of possessions and lives and crops. But give good news to the steadfast.

156 Those who, when a calamity afflicts them, say, "To God we belong, and to Him we will return."

157 Upon these are blessings and mercy from their Lord. These are the guided ones.

158 Safa and Marwa are among the rites of God. Whoever makes the Pilgrimage to the House, or performs the Umrah, commits no error by circulating between them. Whoever volunteers good—God is Appreciative and Cognizant.

159 Those who suppress the proofs and the guidance We have revealed, after We have clarified them to humanity in the Scripture—those—God curses them, and the cursers curse them.

160 Except those who repent, and reform, and proclaim. Those—I will accept their repentance. I am the Acceptor of Repentance, the Merciful.

161 But as for those who reject faith, and die rejecting—those—upon them is the curse of God, and of the angels, and of all humanity.

162 They will remain under it forever, and the torment will not be lightened for them, and they will not be reprieved.

163 Your God is one God. There is no god but He, the Benevolent, the Compassionate.

164 In the creation of the heavens and the earth; in the alternation of night and day; in the ships that sail the oceans for the benefit of mankind; in the water that God sends down from the sky, and revives the earth with it after it had died, and scatters in it all kinds of creatures; in the changing of the winds, and the clouds disposed between the sky and the earth; are signs for people who understand.

165 Yet among the people are those who take other than God as equals to Him. They love them as the love of God. But those who believe have greater love for God. If only the wrongdoers would realize, when they see the torment; that all power is God's, and that God is severe in punishment.

166 Those who were followed will then disown those who followed them, and they will see the retribution, and ties between them will be severed.

167 Those who followed will say, "If only we can have another chance, we will disown them, as they disowned us." Thus God will show them their deeds, as regrets to them, and they will not come out of the Fire.

168 O people! Eat of what is lawful and good on earth, and do not follow the footsteps of Satan. He is to you an open enemy.

169 He commands you to do evil and vice, and to say about God what you do not know.

170 And when it is said to them, "Follow what God has revealed," they say, "We will follow what we found our ancestors following." Even if their ancestors understood nothing, and were not guided?

171 The parable of those who disbelieve is that of someone who calls upon someone who hears nothing except screaming and yelling. Deaf, dumb, and blind—they do not understand.

172 O you who believe! Eat of the good things We have provided for you, and give thanks to God, if it is Him that you serve.

173 He has forbidden you carrion, and blood, and the flesh of swine, and what was dedicated to other than God. But if anyone is compelled, without desiring or exceeding, he commits no sin. God is Forgiving and Merciful.

174 Those who conceal what God revealed in the Book, and exchange it for a small price—those swallow nothing but fire into their bellies. And God will not speak to them on the Day of Resurrection, nor will He purify them, and they will have a painful punishment.

175 It is they who exchange guidance for error, and forgiveness for punishment. But why do they insist on the Fire?

176 That is because God has revealed the Book in truth; and those who differ about the Book are in deep discord.

177 Righteousness does not consist of turning your faces towards the East and the West. But righteous is he who believes in God, and the Last Day, and the angels, and the Scripture, and the prophets. Who gives money, though dear, to near relatives, and orphans, and the needy, and the homeless, and the beggars, and for the freeing of slaves; those who perform the prayers, and pay the obligatory charity, and fulfill their promise when they promise, and patiently persevere in the face of persecution, hardship, and in the time of conflict. These are the sincere; these are the pious.

178 O you who believe! Retaliation for the murdered is ordained upon you: the free for the free, the slave for the slave, the female for the female. But if he is forgiven by his kin, then grant any reasonable demand, and pay with good will. This is a concession from your Lord, and a mercy. But whoever commits aggression after that, a painful torment awaits him.

179 There is life for you in retaliation, O people of understanding, so that you may refrain.

180 It is decreed for you: when death approaches one of you, and he leaves wealth, to make a testament in favor of the parents and the relatives, fairly and correctly—a duty upon the righteous.

181 But whoever changes it after he has heard it, the guilt is upon those who change it. God is All-Hearing, All-Knowing.

182 Should someone suspect bias or injustice on the part of a testator, and then reconciles between them, he commits no sin. God is Forgiving and Merciful.

183 O you who believe! Fasting is prescribed for you, as it was prescribed for those before you, that you may become righteous.

184 For a specified number of days. But whoever among you is sick, or on a journey, then a number of other days. For those who are able: a ransom of feeding a needy person. But whoever volunteers goodness, it is better for him. But to fast is best for you, if you only knew.

185 Ramadan is the month in which the Quran was revealed. Guidance for humanity, and clear portents of guidance, and the Criterion. Whoever of you witnesses the month, shall fast it. But whoever is sick, or on a journey, then a number of other days. God desires ease for you, and does not desire hardship for you, that you may complete the number, and celebrate God for having guided you, so that you may be thankful.

186 And when My servants ask you about Me, I Am near; I answer the call of the caller when he calls on Me. So let them answer Me, and have faith in Me, that they may be rightly guided.

187 Permitted for you is intercourse with your wives on the night of the fast. They are a garment for you, and you are a garment for them. God knows that you used to betray yourselves, but He turned to you and pardoned you. So approach them now, and seek what God has ordained for you, and eat and drink until the white streak of dawn can be distinguished from the black streak. Then complete the fast until nightfall. But do not approach them while you are in retreat at the mosques. These are the limits of God, so do not come near them. God thus clarifies His revelations to the people, that they may attain piety.

188 And do not consume one another's wealth by unjust means, nor offer it as bribes to the officials in order to consume part of other people's wealth illicitly, while you know.

189 They ask you about the crescents. Say, "They are timetables for people, and for the Hajj." It is not virtuous that you approach homes from their backs, but virtue is to be pious. So approach homes from their doors, and observe God, that you may succeed.

190 And fight in the cause of God those who fight you, but do not commit aggression; God does not love the aggressors.

191 And kill them wherever you overtake them, and expel them from where they had expelled you. Oppression is more serious than murder. But do not fight them at the Sacred Mosque, unless they fight you there. If they fight you, then kill them. Such is the retribution of the disbelievers.

192 But if they cease, then God is Forgiving and Merciful.

193 And fight them until there is no oppression, and worship becomes devoted to God alone. But if they cease, then let there be no hostility except against the oppressors.

194 The sacred month for the sacred month; and sacrilege calls for retaliation. Whoever commits aggression against you, retaliate against him in the same measure as he has committed against you. And be conscious of God, and know that God is with the righteous.

195 And spend in the cause of God, and do not throw yourselves with your own hands into ruin, and be charitable. God loves the charitable.

196 And carry out the Hajj and the Umrah for God. But if you are prevented, then whatever is feasible of offerings. And do not shave your heads until the offering has reached its destination. Whoever of you is sick, or has an injury of the head, then redemption of fasting, or charity, or worship. When you are secure: whoever continues the Umrah until the Hajj, then whatever is feasible of offering. But if he lacks the means, then fasting for three days during the Hajj and seven when you have returned, making ten in all. This is for he whose household is not present at the Sacred Mosque. And remain conscious of God, and know that God is stern in retribution.

197 The Hajj is during specific months. Whoever decides to perform the Hajj—there shall be no sexual relations, nor misconduct, nor quarrelling during the Hajj. And whatever good you do, God knows it. And take provisions, but the best provision is righteousness. And be mindful of Me, O people of understanding.

198 You commit no error by seeking bounty from your Lord. When you disperse from Arafat, remember God at the Sacred Landmark. And remember Him as He has guided you. Although, before that, you were of those astray.

199 Then disperse from where the people disperse, and ask God for forgiveness. God is Most Forgiving, Most Merciful.

200 When you have completed your rites, remember God as you remember your parents, or even more. Among the people is he who says, "Our Lord, give us in this world," yet he has no share in the Hereafter.

201 And among them is he who says, "Our Lord, give us goodness in this world, and goodness in the Hereafter, and protect us from the torment of the Fire."

202 These will have a share of what they have earned. God is swift in reckoning.

203 And remember God during the designated days. But whoever hurries on in two days commits no wrong, and whoever stays on commits no wrong—provided he maintains righteousness. And obey God, and know that to Him you will be gathered.

204 Among the people is he whose speech about the worldly life impresses you, and he calls God to witness what is in his heart, while he is the most hostile of adversaries.

205 When he gains power, he strives to spread corruption on earth, destroying properties and lives. God does not like corruption.

206 And when he is told, "Beware of God," his pride leads him to more sin. Hell is enough for him—a dreadful abode.

207 And among the people is he who sells himself seeking God's approval. God is kind towards the servants.

208 O you who believe! Enter into submission, wholeheartedly, and do not follow the footsteps of Satan; he is to you an outright enemy.

209 But if you slip after the proofs have come to you, know that God is Powerful and Wise.

210 Are they waiting for God Himself to come to them in the shadows of the clouds, together with the angels, and thus the matter is settled? All things are returned to God.

211 Ask the Children of Israel how many clear signs We have given them. Whoever alters the blessing of God after it has come to him—God is severe in retribution.

212 Beautified is the life of this world for those who disbelieve, and they ridicule those who believe. But the righteous will be above them on the Day of Resurrection. God provides to whomever He wills without measure.

213 Humanity used to be one community; then God sent the prophets, bringing good news and giving warnings. And He sent down with them the Scripture, with the truth, to judge between people regarding their differences. But none differed over it except those who were given it—after the proofs had come to them—out of mutual envy between them. Then God guided those who believed to the truth they had disputed, in accordance with His will. God guides whom He wills to a straight path.

214 Or do you expect to enter Paradise before the example of those who came before you had reached you? Adversity and hardship had afflicted them, and they were so shaken up, that the Messenger and those who believed with him said, "When is God's victory?" Indeed, God's victory is near.

215 They ask you what they should give. Say, "Whatever charity you give is for the parents, and the relatives, and the orphans, and the poor, and the wayfarer. Whatever good you do, God is aware of it.

216 Fighting is ordained for you, even though you dislike it. But it may be that you dislike something while it is good for you, and it may be that you like something while it is bad for you. God knows, and you do not know.

217 They ask you about fighting during the Holy Month. Say, "Fighting during it is deplorable; but to bar others from God's path, and to disbelieve in Him, and to prevent access to the Holy Mosque, and to expel its people from it, are more deplorable with God. And persecution is more serious than killing. They will not cease to fight you until they turn you back from your religion, if they can. Whoever among you turns back from his religion, and dies a disbeliever—those are they whose works will come to nothing, in this life, and in the Hereafter. Those are the inmates of the Fire, abiding in it forever.

218 Those who believed, and those who migrated and fought for the sake of God—those look forward to God's mercy. God is Forgiving and Merciful.

219 They ask you about intoxicants and gambling. Say, "There is gross sin in them, and some benefits for people, but their sinfulness outweighs their benefit." And they ask you about what they should give: say, "The surplus." Thus God explains the revelations to you, so that you may think.

220 About this world and the next. And they ask you about orphans. Say, "Improvement for them is best. And if you intermix with them, then they are your brethren." God knows the dishonest from the honest. Had God willed, He could have overburdened you. God is Mighty and Wise.

221 Do not marry idolatresses, unless they have believed. A believing maid is better than an idolatress, even if you like her. And do not marry idolaters, unless they have believed. A believing servant is better than an idolater, even if you like him. These call to the Fire, but God calls to the Garden and to forgiveness, by His leave. He makes clear His communications to the people, that they may be mindful.

222 And they ask you about menstruation: say, "It is harmful, so keep away from women during menstruation. And do not approach them until they have become pure. Once they have become pure, approach them in the way God has directed you." God loves the repentant, and He loves those who keep clean."

223 Your women are cultivation for you; so approach your cultivation whenever you like, and send ahead for yourselves. And fear God, and know that you will meet Him. And give good news to the believers.

224 And do not allow your oaths in God's name to hinder you from virtue, and righteousness, and making peace between people. God is Listener and Knower.

225 God does not hold you responsible for your unintentional oaths, but He holds you responsible for your intentions. God is Forgiving and Forbearing.

226 Those who vow abstinence from their wives must wait for four months. But if they reconcile—God is Forgiving and Merciful.

227 And if they resolve to divorce—God is Hearing and Knowing.

228 Divorced women shall wait by themselves for three periods. And it is not lawful for them to conceal what God has created in their wombs, if they believe in God and the Last Day. Meanwhile, their husbands have the better right to take them back, if they desire reconciliation. And women have rights similar to their obligations, according to what is fair. But men have a degree over them. God is Mighty and Wise.

229 Divorce is allowed twice. Then, either honorable retention, or setting free kindly. It is not lawful for you to take back anything you have given them, unless they fear that they cannot maintain God's limits. If you fear that they cannot maintain God's limits, then there is no blame on them if she sacrifices something for her release. These are God's limits, so do not transgress them. Those who transgress God's limits are the unjust.

230 If he divorces her, she shall not be lawful for him again until she has married another husband. If the latter divorces her, then there is no blame on them for reuniting, provided they think they can maintain God's limits. These are God's limits; He makes them clear to people who know.

231 When you divorce women, and they have reached their term, either retain them amicably, or release them amicably. But do not retain them to hurt them and commit aggression. Whoever does that has wronged himself. And do not take God's revelations for a joke. And remember God's favor to you, and that He revealed to you the Scripture and Wisdom to teach you. And fear God, and know that God is aware of everything.

232 When you divorce women, and they have reached their term, do not prevent them from marrying their husbands, provided they agree on fair terms. Thereby is advised whoever among you believes in God and the Last Day. That is better and more decent for you. God knows, and you do not know.

233 Mothers may nurse their infants for two whole years, for those who desire to complete the nursing-period. It is the duty of the father to provide for them and clothe them in a proper manner. No soul shall be burdened beyond its capacity. No mother shall be harmed on account of her child, and no father shall be harmed on account of his child. The same duty rests upon the heir. If the couple desire weaning, by mutual consent and consultation, they commit no error by doing so. You commit no error by hiring nursing-mothers, as long as you pay them fairly. And be wary of God, and know that God is Seeing of what you do.

234 As for those among you who die and leave widows behind, their widows shall wait by themselves for four months and ten days. When they have reached their term, there is no blame on you regarding what they might honorably do with themselves. God is fully acquainted with what you do.

235 You commit no error by announcing your engagement to women, or by keeping it to yourselves. God knows that you will be thinking about them. But do not meet them secretly, unless you have something proper to say. And do not confirm the marriage tie until the writing is fulfilled. And know that God knows what is in your souls, so beware of Him. And know that God is Forgiving and Forbearing.

236 You commit no error by divorcing women before having touched them, or before having set the dowry for them. And compensate them—the wealthy according to his means, and the poor according to his means—with a fair compensation, a duty upon the doers of good.

237 If you divorce them before you have touched them, but after you had set the dowry for them, give them half of what you specified—unless they forego the right, or the one in whose hand is the marriage contract foregoes it. But to forego is nearer to piety. And do not forget generosity between one another. God is seeing of everything you do.

238 Guard your prayers, and the middle prayer, and stand before God in devotion.

239 But if you are in fear, then on foot, or riding. And when you are safe, remember God, as He taught you what you did not know.

240 Those of you who die and leave wives behind—a will shall provide their wives with support for a year, provided they do not leave. If they leave, you are not to blame for what they do with themselves, provided it is reasonable. God is Mighty and Wise.

241 And divorced women shall be provided for, equitably—a duty upon the righteous.

242 God thus explains His revelations to you, so that you may understand.

243 Have you not considered those who fled their homes, by the thousands, fearful of death? God said to them, "Die." Then He revived them. God is Gracious towards the people, but most people are not appreciative.

244 Fight in the cause of God, and know that God is Hearing and Knowing.

245 Who is he who will offer God a generous loan, so He will multiply it for him manifold? God receives and amplifies, and to Him you will be returned.

246 Have you not considered the notables of the Children of Israel after Moses? When they said to a prophet of theirs, "Appoint a king for us, and we will fight in the cause of God." He said, "Is it possible that, if fighting was ordained for you, you would not fight?" They said, "Why would we not fight in the cause of God, when we were driven out of our homes, along with our children?" But when fighting was ordained for them, they turned away, except for a few of them. But God is aware of the wrongdoers.

247 Their prophet said to them, "God has appointed Saul to be your king." They said, "How can he have authority over us, when we are more worthy of authority than he, and he was not given plenty of wealth?" He said, "God has chosen him over you, and has increased him in knowledge and stature." God bestows His sovereignty upon whomever He wills. God is Embracing and Knowing.

248 And their prophet said to them, "The proof of his kingship is that the Ark will be restored to you, bringing tranquility from your Lord, and relics left by the family of Moses and the family of Aaron. It will be carried by the angels. In that is a sign for you, if you are believers."

249 When Saul set out with the troops, he said, "God will be testing you with a river. Whoever drinks from it does not belong with me. But whoever does not drink from it, does belong with me, except for whoever scoops up a little with his hand." But they drank from it, except for a few of them. Then, when he crossed it, he and those who believed with him, they said, "We have no strength to face Goliath and his troops today." But those who knew that they would meet God said, "How many a small group has defeated a large group by God's will. God is with the steadfast."

250 And when they confronted Goliath and his troops, they said, "Our Lord, pour down patience on us, and strengthen our foothold, and support us against the faithless people."

251 And they defeated them by God's leave, and David killed Goliath, and God gave him sovereignty and wisdom, and taught him as He willed. Were it not for God restraining the people, some by means of others, the earth would have gone to ruin. But God is gracious towards mankind.

252 These are God's revelations, which We recite to you in truth. You are one of the messengers.

253 These messengers: We gave some advantage over others. To some of them God spoke directly, and some He raised in rank. We gave Jesus son of Mary the clear miracles, and We strengthened him with the Holy Spirit. Had God willed, those who succeeded them would not have fought one another, after the clear signs had come to them; but they disputed; some of them believed, and some of them disbelieved. Had God willed, they would not have fought one another; but God does whatever He desires.

254 O you who believe! Spend from what We have given you, before a Day comes in which there is neither trading, nor friendship, nor intercession. The disbelievers are the wrongdoers.

255 God! There is no god except He, the Living, the Everlasting. Neither slumber overtakes Him, nor sleep. To Him belongs everything in the heavens and everything on earth. Who is he that can intercede with Him except with His permission? He knows what is before them, and what is behind them; and they cannot grasp any of His knowledge, except as He wills. His Throne extends over the heavens and the earth, and their preservation does not burden Him. He is the Most High, the Great.

256 There shall be no compulsion in religion; the right way has become distinct from the wrong way. Whoever renounces evil and believes in God has grasped the most trustworthy handle; which does not break. God is Hearing and Knowing.

257 God is the Lord of those who believe; He brings them out of darkness and into light. As for those who disbelieve, their lords are the evil ones; they bring them out of light and into darkness—these are the inmates of the Fire, in which they will abide forever.

258 Have you not considered him who argued with Abraham about his Lord, because God had given him sovereignty? Abraham said, "My Lord is He who gives life and causes death." He said, "I give life and cause death." Abraham said, "God brings the sun from the East, so bring it from the West," so the blasphemer was confounded. God does not guide the wrongdoing people.

259 Or like him who passed by a town collapsed on its foundations. He said, "How can God revive this after its demise?" Thereupon God caused him to die for a hundred years, and then resurrected him. He said, "For how long have you tarried?" He said, "I have tarried for a day, or part of a day." He said, "No. You have tarried for a hundred years. Now look at your food and your drink—it has not spoiled—and look at your donkey. We will make you a wonder for mankind. And look at the bones, how We arrange them, and then clothe them with flesh." So when it became clear to him, he said, "I know that God has power over all things."

260 And when Abraham said, "My Lord, show me how You give life to the dead." He said, "Have you not believed?" He said, "Yes, but to put my heart at ease." He said, "Take four birds, and incline them to yourself, then place a part on each hill, then call to them; and they will come rushing to you. And know that God is Powerful and Wise."

261 The parable of those who spend their wealth in God's way is that of a grain that produces seven spikes; in each spike is a hundred grains. God multiplies for whom He wills. God is Bounteous and Knowing.

262 Those who spend their wealth in the way of God, and then do not follow up what they spent with reminders of their generosity or with insults, will have their reward with their Lord—they have nothing to fear, nor shall they grieve.

263 Kind words and forgiveness are better than charity followed by insults. God is Rich and Clement.

264 O you who believe! Do not nullify your charitable deeds with reminders and hurtful words, like him who spends his wealth to be seen by the people, and does not believe in God and the Last Day. His likeness is that of a smooth rock covered with soil: a downpour strikes it, and leaves it bare—they gain nothing from their efforts. God does not guide the disbelieving people.

265 And the parable of those who spend their wealth seeking God's approval, and to strengthen their souls, is that of a garden on a hillside. If heavy rain falls on it, its produce is doubled; and if no heavy rain falls, then dew is enough. God is seeing of everything you do.

266 Would anyone of you like to have a garden of palms and vines, under which rivers flow—with all kinds of fruit in it for him, and old age has stricken him, and he has weak children—then a tornado with fire batters it, and it burns down? Thus God makes clear the signs for you, so that you may reflect.

267 O you who believe! Give of the good things you have earned, and from what We have produced for you from the earth. And do not pick the inferior things to give away, when you yourselves would not accept it except with eyes closed. And know that God is Sufficient and Praiseworthy.

268 Satan promises you poverty, and urges you to immorality; but God promises you forgiveness from Himself, and grace. God is Embracing and Knowing.

269 He gives wisdom to whomever He wills. Whoever is given wisdom has been given much good. But none pays heed except those with insight.

270 Whatever charity you give, or a pledge you fulfill, God knows it. The wrongdoers have no helpers.

271 If you give charity openly, that is good. But if you keep it secret, and give it to the needy in private, that is better for you. It will atone for some of your misdeeds. God is cognizant of what you do.

272 Their guidance is not your responsibility, but God guides whom He wills. Any charity you give is for your own good. Any charity you give shall be for the sake of God. Any charity you give will be repaid to you in full, and you will not be wronged.

273 It is for the poor; those who are restrained in the way of God, and unable to travel in the land. The unaware would think them rich, due to their dignity. You will recognize them by their features. They do not ask from people insistently. Whatever charity you give, God is aware of it.

274 Those who spend their wealth by night and day, privately and publicly, will receive their reward from their Lord. They have nothing to fear, nor shall they grieve.

275 Those who swallow usury will not rise, except as someone driven mad by Satan's touch. That is because they say, "Commerce is like usury." But God has permitted commerce, and has forbidden usury. Whoever, on receiving advice from his Lord, refrains, may keep his past earnings, and his case rests with God. But whoever resumes—these are the dwellers of the Fire, wherein they will abide forever.

276 God condemns usury, and He blesses charities. God does not love any sinful ingrate.

277 Those who believe, and do good deeds, and pray regularly, and give charity—they will have their reward with their Lord; they will have no fear, nor shall they grieve.

278 O you who believe! Fear God, and forgo what remains of usury, if you are believers.

279 If you do not, then take notice of a war by God and His Messenger. But if you repent, you may keep your capital, neither wronging, nor being wronged.

280 But if he is in hardship, then deferment until a time of ease. But to remit it as charity is better for you, if you only knew.

281 And guard yourselves against a Day when you will be returned to God; then each soul will be rewarded fully for what it has earned, and they will not be wronged.

282 O you who believe! When you incur debt among yourselves for a certain period of time, write it down. And have a scribe write in your presence, in all fairness. And let no scribe refuse to write, as God has taught him. So let him write, and let the debtor dictate. And let him fear God, his Lord, and diminish nothing from it. But if the debtor is mentally deficient, or weak, or unable to dictate, then let his guardian dictate with honesty. And call to witness two men from among you. If two men are not available, then one man and two women whose testimony is acceptable to all—if one of them fails to remember, the other would remind her. Witnesses must not refuse when called upon. And do not think it too trivial to write down, whether small or large, including the time of repayment. That is more equitable with God, and stronger as evidence, and more likely to prevent doubt—except in the case of a spot transaction between you—then there is no blame on you if you do not write it down. And let there be witnesses whenever you conclude a contract, and let no harm be done to either scribe or witness. If you do that, it is corruption on your part. And fear God. God teaches you. God is aware of everything.

283 If you are on a journey, and cannot find a scribe, then a security deposit should be handed over. But if you trust one another, let the trustee fulfill his trust, and let him fear God, his Lord. And do not conceal testimony. Whoever conceals it is sinner at heart. God is aware of what you do.

284 To God belongs everything in the heavens and the earth. Whether you reveal what is within your selves, or conceal it, God will call you to account for it. He forgives whom He wills, and He punishes whom He wills. God is Able to do all things.

285 The Messenger has believed in what was revealed to him from his Lord, as did the believers. They all have believed in God, and His angels, and His scriptures, and His messengers: "We make no distinction between any of His messengers." And they say, "We hear and we obey. Your forgiveness, our Lord. To you is the destiny."

286 God does not burden any soul beyond its capacity. To its credit is what it earns, and against it is what it commits. "Our Lord, do not condemn us if we forget or make a mistake. Our Lord, do not burden us as You have burdened those before us. Our Lord, do not burden us with more than we have strength to bear; and pardon us, and forgive us, and have mercy on us. You are our Lord and Master, so help us against the disbelieving people."

Family of Imran (Ali 'Imran)

In the name of God, the Gracious, the Merciful.

1 Alif, Lam, Meem.

2 God, there is no god but He, the Living, the Eternal.

3 He sent down to you the Book with the Truth, confirming what came before it; and He sent down the Torah and the Gospel.

4 Aforetime, as guidance for mankind; and He sent down the Criterion. Those who have rejected God's signs will have a severe punishment. God is Mighty, Able to take revenge.

5 Nothing is hidden from God, on earth or in the heaven.

6 It is He who forms you in the wombs as He wills. There is no god except He, the Almighty, the Wise.

7 It is He who revealed to you the Book. Some of its verses are definitive; they are the foundation of the Book, and others are unspecific. As for those in whose hearts is deviation, they follow the unspecific part, seeking dissent, and seeking to derive an interpretation. But none knows its interpretation except God and those firmly rooted in knowledge say, "We believe in it; all is from our Lord." But none recollects except those with understanding.

8 "Our Lord, do not cause our hearts to swerve after You have guided us, and bestow on us mercy from Your presence; You are the Giver."

9 "Our Lord, You will gather the people for a Day in which there is no doubt." God will never break His promise.

10 As for those who disbelieve, neither their wealth nor their children will avail them anything against God. These will be fuel for the Fire.

11 Like the behavior of Pharaoh's people and those before them. They rejected Our signs, so God seized them for their sins. God is Strict in retribution.

12 Say to those who disbelieve, "You will be defeated, and rounded up into Hell—an awful resting-place."

13 There was a sign for you in the two parties that met. One party fighting in the way of God, and the other was disbelieving. They saw them with their own eyes twice their number. But God supports with His help whomever He wills. In that is a lesson for those with insight.

14 Adorned for the people is the love of desires, such as women, and children, and piles upon piles of gold and silver, and branded horses, and livestock, and fields. These are the conveniences of the worldly life, but with God lies the finest resort.

15 Say, "Shall I inform you of something better than that? For those who are righteous, with their Lord are Gardens beneath which rivers flow, where they will remain forever, and purified spouses, and acceptance from God." God is Observant of the servants.

16 Those who say, "Our Lord, we have believed, so forgive us our sins, and save us from the suffering of the Fire."

17 The patient, and the truthful, and the reverent, and the charitable, and the seekers of forgiveness at dawn.

18 God bears witness that there is no god but He, as do the angels, and those endowed with knowledge—upholding justice. There is no god but He, the Mighty, the Wise.

19 Religion with God is Islam. Those to whom the Scripture was given differed only after knowledge came to them, out of envy among themselves. Whoever rejects the signs of God—God is quick to take account.

20 If they argue with you, say, "I have surrendered myself to God, and those who follow me." And say to those who were given the Scripture, and to the unlearned, "Have you surrendered?" If they have surrendered, then they are guided; but if they turn away, then your duty is to convey. God is Seeing of the servants.

21 As for those who defy God's revelations, and kill the prophets unjustly, and kill those who advocate justice among the people—promise them a painful retribution.

22 They are those whose deeds will come to nothing, in this world and in the Hereafter; and they will have no saviors.

23 Have you not considered those who were given a share of the Scripture, as they were called to the Scripture of God to arbitrate between them; then some of them turned back, and declined?

24 That is because they said, "The Fire will not touch us except for a limited number of days." They have been misled in their religion by the lies they fabricated.

25 How about when We gather them for a Day in which there is no doubt, and each soul will be paid in full for what it has earned, and they will not be wronged?

26 Say, "O God, Owner of Sovereignty. You grant sovereignty to whom You will, and You strip sovereignty from whom you will. You honor whom you will, and You humiliate whom you will. In Your hand is all goodness. You are Capable of all things."

27 "You merge the night into the day, and You merge the day into the night; and you bring the living out of the dead, and You bring the dead out of the living; and You provide for whom you will without measure."

28 Believers are not to take disbelievers for friends instead of believers. Whoever does that has nothing to do with God, unless it is to protect your own selves against them. God warns you to beware of Him. To God is the destiny.

29 Say, "Whether you conceal what is in your hearts, or disclose it, God knows it." He knows everything in the heavens and the earth. God is Powerful over everything.

30 On the Day when every soul finds all the good it has done presented. And as for the evil it has done, it will wish there were a great distance between them. God cautions you of Himself. God is Kind towards the servants.

31 Say, "If you love God, then follow me, and God will love you, and will forgive you your sins." God is Forgiving and Merciful.

32 Say, "Obey God and the Messenger." But if they turn away—God does not love the faithless.

33 God chose Adam, and Noah, and the family of Abraham, and the family of Imran, over all mankind.

34 Offspring one of the other. God is Hearer and Knower.

35 The wife of Imran said, "My Lord, I have vowed to You what is in my womb, dedicated, so accept from me; You are the Hearer and Knower."

36 And when she delivered her, she said, "My Lord, I have delivered a female," and God was well aware of what she has delivered, "and the male is not like the female, and I have named her Mary, and have commended her and her descendants to Your protection, from Satan the outcast."

37 Her Lord accepted her with a gracious reception, and brought her a beautiful upbringing, and entrusted her to the care of Zechariah. Whenever Zechariah entered upon her in the sanctuary, he found her with provision. He said,

"O Mary, where did you get this from?" She said, "It is from God; God provides to whom He wills without reckoning."

38 Thereupon Zechariah prayed to his Lord; he said, "My Lord, bestow on me good offspring from Your presence; You are the Hearer of Prayers."

39 Then the angels called out to him, as he stood praying in the sanctuary: "God gives you good news of John; confirming a Word from God, and honorable, and moral, and a prophet; one of the upright."

40 He said, "My Lord, how will I have a son, when old age has overtaken me, and my wife is barren?" He said, "Even so, God does whatever He wills."

41 He said, "My Lord, give me a sign." He said, "Your sign is that you shall not speak to the people for three days, except by gestures. And remember your Lord much, and praise in the evening and the morning."

42 The angels said, "O Mary, God has chosen you, and has purified you. He has chosen you over all the women of the world.

43 "O Mary, be devoted to your Lord, and bow down, and kneel with those who kneel."

44 These are accounts from the Unseen, which We reveal to you. You were not with them when they cast their lots as to which of them would take charge of Mary; nor were you with them as they quarreled.

45 The Angels said, "O Mary, God gives you good news of a Word from Him. His name is the Messiah, Jesus, son of Mary, well-esteemed in this world and the next, and one of the nearest.

46 He will speak to the people from the crib, and in adulthood, and will be one of the righteous."

47 She said, "My Lord, how can I have a child, when no man has touched me?" He said, "It will be so. God creates whatever He wills. To have anything done, He only says to it, 'Be,' and it is."

48 And He will teach him the Scripture and wisdom, and the Torah and the Gospel.

49 A messenger to the Children of Israel: "I have come to you with a sign from your Lord. I make for you out of clay the figure of a bird; then I breathe into it, and it becomes a bird by God's leave. And I heal the blind and the leprous, and I revive the dead, by God's leave. And I inform you concerning what you eat, and what you store in your homes. In that is a sign for you, if you are believers."

50 "And verifying what lies before me of the Torah, and to make lawful for you some of what was forbidden to you. I have come to you with a sign from your Lord; so fear God, and obey me."

51 "God is my Lord and your Lord, so worship Him. That is a straight path."

52 When Jesus sensed disbelief on their part, he said, "Who are my allies towards God?" The disciples said, "We are God's allies; we have believed in God, and bear witness that we submit."

53 "Our Lord, we have believed in what You have revealed, and we have followed the Messenger, so count us among the witnesses."

54 They planned, and God planned; but God is the Best of planners.

55 God said, "O Jesus, I am terminating your life, and raising you to Me, and clearing you of those who disbelieve. And I will make those who follow you superior to those who disbelieve, until the Day of Resurrection. Then to Me is your return; then I will judge between you regarding what you were disputing.

56 As for those who disbelieve, I will punish them with a severe punishment, in this world and the next, and they will have no helpers.

57 And as for those who believe and do good works, He will give them their rewards in full. God does not love the unjust."

58 This is what We recite to you of the Verses and the Wise Reminder.

59 The likeness of Jesus in God's sight is that of Adam: He created him from dust, then said to him, "Be," and he was.

60 The truth is from your Lord, so do not be of those who doubt.

61 And if anyone disputes with you about him, after the knowledge that has come to you, say, "Come, let us call our children and your children, and our women and your women, and ourselves and yourselves, and let us invoke God's curse on the liars."

62 This is the narrative of truth: there is no god but God. God is the Mighty, the Wise.

63 But if they turn away—God knows the corrupt.

64 Say, "O People of the Book, come to terms common between us and you: that we worship none but God, and that we associate nothing with Him, and that none of us takes others as lords besides God." And if they turn away, say, "Bear witness that we have submitted."

65 O People of the Book! Why do you argue about Abraham, when the Torah and the Gospel were not revealed until after him? Will you not reason?

66 Here you are—you argue about things you know, but why do you argue about things you do not know? God knows, and you do not know.

67 Abraham was neither a Jew nor a Christian, but he was a Monotheist, a Muslim. And he was not of the Polytheists.

68 The people most deserving of Abraham are those who followed him, and this prophet, and those who believe. God is the Guardian of the believers.

69 A party of the People of the Book would love to lead you astray, but they only lead themselves astray, and they do not realize it.

70 O People of the Book! Why do you reject the revelations of God, even as you witness?

71 O People of the Book! Why do you confound the truth with falsehood, and knowingly conceal the truth?

72 Some of the People of the Book say, "Believe in what was revealed to the believers at the beginning of the day, and reject it at its end, so that they may return."

73 And trust none except those who follow your religion." Say, "Guidance is God's guidance. If someone is given the like of what you were given, or they argue with you before your Lord, say, "All grace is in God's hand; He gives it to whomever He wills." God is Bounteous and Knowing.

74 He specifies His mercy for whomever He wills. God is Possessor of Sublime Grace.

75 Among the People of the Book is he, who, if you entrust him with a heap of gold, he will give it back to you. And among them is he, who, if you entrust him with a single coin, he will not give it back to you, unless you keep after him. That is because they say, "We are under no obligation towards the gentiles." They tell lies about God, and they know it.

76 Indeed, whoever fulfills his commitments and maintains piety—God loves the pious.

77 Those who exchange the covenant of God, and their vows, for a small price, will have no share in the Hereafter, and God will not speak to them, nor will He look at them on the Day of Resurrection, nor will He purify them. They will have a painful punishment.

78 And among them are those who twist the Scripture with their tongues, that you may think it from the Scripture, when it is not from the Scripture. And they say, "It is from God," when it is not from God. They tell lies and attribute them to God, knowingly.

79 No person to whom God has given the Scripture, and wisdom, and prophethood would ever say to the people, "Be my worshipers rather than God's." Rather, "Be people of the Lord, according to the Scripture you teach, and the teachings you learn."

80 Nor would he command you to take the angels and the prophets as lords. Would he command you to infidelity after you have submitted?

81 God received the covenant of the prophets, "Inasmuch as I have given you of scripture and wisdom; should a messenger come to you verifying what you have, you shall believe in him, and support him." He said, "Do you affirm My covenant and take it upon yourselves?" They said, "We affirm it." He said, "Then bear witness, and I am with you among the witnesses."

82 Whoever turns away after that—these are the deceitful.

83 Do they desire other than the religion of God, when to Him has submitted everything in the heavens and the earth, willingly or unwillingly, and to Him they will be returned?

84 Say, "We believe in God, and in what was revealed to us; and in what was revealed to Abraham, and Ishmael, and Isaac, and Jacob, and the Patriarchs; and in what was given to Moses, and Jesus, and the prophets from their Lord. We make no distinction between any of them, and to Him we submit."

85 Whoever seeks other than Islam as a religion, it will not be accepted from him, and in the Hereafter he will be among the losers.

86 How will God guide a people who disbelieved after having believed, and had witnessed that the Messenger is true, and the clear proofs had come to them? God does not guide the unjust people.

87 Those—their penalty is that upon them falls the curse of God, and of the angels, and of all mankind.

88 Remaining in it eternally, without their punishment being eased from them, and without being reprieved.

89 Except those who repent afterwards, and reform; for God is Forgiving and Merciful.

90 As for those who disbelieve after having believed, then plunge deeper into disbelief, their repentance will not be accepted; these are the lost.

91 As for those who disbelieve and die disbelievers, even the earth full of gold would not be accepted from any of them, were he to offer it for ransom. These will have a painful torment, and will have no saviors.

92 You will not attain virtuous conduct until you give of what you cherish. Whatever you give away, God is aware of it.

93 All food was permissible to the Children of Israel, except what Israel forbade for itself before the Torah was revealed. Say, "Bring the Torah, and read it, if you are truthful."

94 Whoever forges lies about God after that—these are the unjust.

95 Say, "God has spoken the truth, so follow the religion of Abraham the Monotheist; he was not a Pagan."

96 The first house established for mankind is the one at Bekka; blessed, and guidance for all people.

97 In it are evident signs; the Station of Abraham. Whoever enters it attains security. Pilgrimage to the House is a duty to God for all who can make the journey. But as for those who refuse—God is Independent of the worlds.

98 Say, "O People of the Scripture, why do you reject the Revelations of God, when God witnesses what you do?"

99 Say, "O People of the Scripture, why do you hinder from God's path those who believe, seeking to distort it, even though you are witnesses? God is not unaware of what you do."

100 O you who believe! If you obey a party of those who were given the Scripture, they will turn you, after your belief, into disbelievers.

101 And how could you disbelieve, when God's revelations are being recited to you, and among you is His Messenger? Whoever cleaves to God has been guided to a straight path.

102 O you who believe! Revere God with due reverence, and do not die except as Muslims.

103 And hold fast to the rope of God, altogether, and do not become divided. And remember God's blessings upon you; how you were enemies, and He reconciled your hearts, and by His grace you became brethren. And you were on the brink of a pit of fire, and He saved you from it. God thus clarifies His revelations for you, so that you may be guided.

104 And let there be among you a community calling to virtue, and advocating righteousness, and deterring from evil. These are the successful.

105 And do not be like those who separated and disputed after the clear proofs came to them; for them is a great punishment.

106 On the Day when some faces will be whitened, and some faces will be blackened. As for those whose faces are blackened: "Did you disbelieve after your belief?" Then taste the punishment for having disbelieved.

107 But as for those whose faces are whitened: they are in God's mercy, remaining in it forever.

108 These are the revelations of God. We recite them to you in truth. God desires no injustice for mankind.

109 To God belongs everything in the heavens and everything on earth, and to God all events are referred.

110 You are the best community that ever emerged for humanity: you advocate what is moral, and forbid what is immoral, and believe in God. Had the People of the Scripture believed, it would have been better for them. Among them are the believers, but most of them are sinners.

111 They will do you no harm, beyond insulting you. And if they fight you, they will turn around and flee, then they will not be helped.

112 They shall be humiliated wherever they are encountered, except through a rope from God, and a rope from the people; and they incurred wrath from God, and were stricken with misery. That is because they rejected God's revelations, and killed the prophets unjustly. That is because they rebelled and committed aggression.

113 They are not alike. Among the People of the Scripture is a community that is upright; they recite God's revelations throughout the night, and they prostrate themselves.

114 They believe in God and the Last Day, and advocate righteousness and forbid evil, and are quick to do good deeds. These are among the righteous.

115 Whatever good they do, they will not be denied it. God knows the righteous.

116 As for those who disbelieve, neither their possessions nor their children will avail them anything against God. These are the inhabitants of the Fire, abiding therein forever.

117 The parable of what they spend in this worldly life is that of a frosty wind that strikes the harvest of a people who have wronged their souls, and destroys it. God did not wrong them, but they wronged their own selves.

118 O you who believe! Do not befriend outsiders who never cease to wish you harm. They love to see you suffer. Hatred has already appeared from their mouths, but what their hearts conceal is worse. We have made the messages clear for you, if you understand.

119 There you are, you love them, but they do not love you, and you believe in the entire scripture. And when they meet you, they say, "We believe;" but when they are alone, they bite their fingers in rage at you. Say, "Die in your rage; God knows what is within the hearts."

120 If something good happens to you, it upsets them; but if something bad befalls you, they rejoice at it. But if you persevere and maintain righteousness, their schemes will not harm you at all. God comprehends what they do.

121 Remember when you left your home in the morning, to assign battle-positions for the believers. God is Hearing and Knowing.

122 When two groups among you almost faltered, but God was their Protector. So in God let the believers put their trust.

123 God had given you victory at Badr, when you were weak. So fear God, that you may be thankful.

124 When you said to the believers, "Is it not enough for you that your Lord has reinforced you with three thousand angels, sent down?"

125 It is; but if you persevere and remain cautious, and they attack you suddenly, your Lord will reinforce you with five thousand angels, well trained.

126 God made it but a message of hope for you, and to reassure your hearts thereby. Victory comes only from God the Almighty, the Wise.

127 He thus cuts off a section of those who disbelieved, or subdues them, so they retreat disappointed.

128 It is no concern of yours whether He redeems them or punishes them. They are wrongdoers.

129 To God belongs everything in the heavens and the earth. He forgives whom He wills, and He punishes whom He wills. God is Most Forgiving, Most Merciful.

130 O you who believe! Do not feed on usury, compounded over and over, and fear God, so that you may prosper.

131 And guard yourselves against the Fire that is prepared for the disbelievers.

132 And obey God and the Messenger, that you may obtain mercy.

133 And race towards forgiveness from your Lord, and a Garden as wide as the heavens and the earth, prepared for the righteous.

134 Those who give in prosperity and adversity, and those who restrain anger, and those who forgive people. God loves the doers of good.

135 And those who, when they commit an indecency or wrong themselves, remember God and ask forgiveness for their sins—and who forgives sins except God? And they do not persist in their wrongdoing while they know.

136 Those—their reward is forgiveness from their Lord, and gardens beneath which rivers flow, abiding therein forever. How excellent is the reward of the workers.

137 Many societies have passed away before you. So travel the earth and note the fate of the deniers.

138 This is a proclamation to humanity, and guidance, and advice for the righteous.

139 And do not waver, nor feel remorse. You are the superior ones, if you are believers.

140 If a wound afflicts you, a similar wound has afflicted the others. Such days We alternate between the people, that God may know those who believe, and take martyrs from among you. God does not love the evildoers.

141 So that God may prove those who believe, and eliminate the disbelievers.

142 Or do you expect to enter Paradise, before God has distinguished those among you who strive, and before He has distinguished the steadfast?

143 You used to wish for death before you have faced it. Now you have seen it before your own eyes.

144 Muhammad is no more than a messenger. Messengers have passed on before him. If he dies or gets killed, will you turn on your heels? He who turns on his heels will not harm God in any way. And God will reward the appreciative.

145 No soul can die except by God's leave, at a predetermined time. Whoever desires the reward of the world, We will give him some of it; and whoever desires the reward of the Hereafter, We will give him some of it; and We will reward the appreciative.

146 How many a prophet fought alongside him numerous godly people? They did not waver for what afflicted them in the cause of God, nor did they weaken, nor did they give in. God loves those who endure.

147 Their only words were, "Our Lord, forgive us our offences, and our excesses in our conduct, and strengthen our foothold, and help us against the disbelieving people."

148 So God gave them the reward of this world, and the excellent reward of the Hereafter. God loves the doers of good.

149 O you who believe! If you obey those who disbelieve, they will turn you back on your heels, and you end up losers.

150 God is your Master, and He is the Best of Helpers.

151 We will throw terror into the hearts of those who disbelieve, because they attribute to God partners for which He revealed no sanction. Their lodging is the Fire. Miserable is the lodging of the evildoers.

152 God has fulfilled His promise to you, and you defeated them by His leave; until when you faltered, and disputed the command, and disobeyed after He had shown you what you like. Some of you want this world, and some of you want the next. Then He turned you away from them, to test you; but He pardoned you. God is Gracious towards the believers.

153 Remember when you fled, not caring for anyone, even though the Messenger was calling you from your rear. Then He repaid you with sorrow upon sorrow, so that you would not grieve over what you missed, or for what afflicted you. God is Informed of what you do.

154 Then after the setback, He sent down security upon you. Slumber overcame some of you, while others cared only for themselves, thinking of God thoughts that were untrue—thoughts of ignorance—saying, "Is anything up to us?" Say, "Everything is up to God." They conceal within themselves what they do not reveal to you. And they say, "If it was up to us, none of us would have been killed here." Say, "Even if you Had stayed in your homes, those destined to be killed would have marched into their death beds." God thus tests what is in your minds, and purifies what is in your hearts. God knows what the hearts contain.

155 Those of you who turned back on the day when the two armies clashed—it was Satan who caused them to backslide, on account of some of what they have earned. But God has forgiven them. God is Forgiving and Prudent.

156 O you who believe! Do not be like those who disbelieved, and said of their brethren who marched in the land, or went on the offensive, "Had they stayed with us, they would not have died or been killed." So that God may make it a cause of regret in their hearts. God gives life and causes death. God is Seeing of what you do.

157 If you are killed in the cause of God, or die—forgiveness and mercy from God are better than what they hoard.

158 If you die, or are killed—to God you will be gathered up.

159 It is by of grace from God that you were gentle with them. Had you been harsh, hardhearted, they would have dispersed from around you. So pardon them, and ask forgiveness for them, and consult them in the conduct of affairs. And when you make a decision, put your trust in God; God loves the trusting.

160 If God supports you, there is none who can overcome you. But if He fails you, who is there to help you after Him? So in God let the believers put their trust.

161 It is not for a prophet to act dishonestly. Whoever acts dishonestly will bring his dishonesty on the Day of Resurrection. Then every soul will be paid in full for what it has earned, and they will not be wronged.

162 Is someone who pursues God's approval the same as someone who incurs God's wrath and his refuge is Hell—the miserable destination?

163 They have different ranks with God, and God is Seeing of what they do.

164 God has blessed the believers, as He raised up among them a messenger from among themselves, who recites to them His revelations, and purifies them, and teaches them the Scripture and wisdom; although before that they were in evident error.

165 And when a calamity befell you, even after you had inflicted twice as much, you said, "How is this?" Say, "It is from your own selves." God is Able to do all things.

166 What befell you on the day the two armies clashed was with God's permission; that He may know the believers.

167 And that He may know the hypocrites. And it was said to them, "Come, fight in the cause of God, or contribute." They said, "If we knew how to fight, we would have followed you." On that day they were closer to infidelity than they were to faith. They say with their mouths what is not in their hearts; but God knows what they hide.

168 Those who said of their brethren, as they stayed behind, "Had they obeyed us, they would not have been killed." Say, "Then avert death from yourselves, if you are truthful."

169 Do not consider those killed in the cause of God as dead. In fact, they are alive, at their Lord, well provided for.

170 Delighting in what God has given them out of His grace, and happy for those who have not yet joined them; that they have nothing to fear, nor will they grieve.

171 They rejoice in grace from God, and bounty, and that God will not waste the reward of the faithful.

172 Those who responded to God and the Messenger, despite the persecution they had suffered. For the virtuous and the pious among them is a great reward.

173 Those to whom the people have said, "The people have mobilized against you, so fear them." But this only increased them in faith, and they said, "God is enough for us; He is the Excellent Protector."

174 So they came back with grace from God, and bounty, and no harm having touched them. They pursued what pleases God. God possesses immense grace.

175 That is only Satan frightening his partisans; so do not fear them, but fear Me, if you are believers.

176 And do not be saddened by those who rush into disbelief. They will not harm God in the least. God desires to give them no share in the Hereafter. A terrible torment awaits them.

177 Those who exchange blasphemy for faith will not harm God in the least. A painful torment awaits them.

178 Those who disbelieve should not assume that We respite them for their own good. In fact, We only respite them so that they may increase in sinfulness. A humiliating torment awaits them.

179 God will not leave the believers as you are, without distinguishing the wicked from the sincere. Nor will God inform you of the future, but God elects from among His messengers whom He wills. So believe in God and His messengers. If you believe and practice piety, you will have a splendid reward.

180 Those who withhold what God has given them of his bounty should not assume that is good for them. In fact, it is bad for them. They will be encircled by their hoardings on the Day of Resurrection. To God belongs the inheritance of the heavens and the earth, and God is well acquainted with what you do.

181 God has heard the statement of those who said, "God is poor, and we are rich." We will write down what they said, and their wrongful killing of the prophets; and We will say, "Taste the torment of the burning."

182 "This is on account of what your hands have forwarded, and because God is not unjust towards the creatures."

183 Those who said, "God has made a covenant with us, that we shall not believe in any messenger unless he brings us an offering to be consumed by fire." Say, "Messengers have come to you before me with proofs, and with what you asked for; so why did you assassinate them, if you are truthful?"

184 If they accuse you of lying, messengers before you were accused of lying. They came with the proofs, and the Psalms, and the Illuminating Scripture.

185 Every soul will have a taste of death, and you will receive your recompense on the Day of Resurrection. Whoever is swayed from the Fire, and admitted to Paradise, has won. The life of this world is merely enjoyment of delusion.

186 You will be tested through your possessions and your persons; and you will hear from those who received the Scripture before you, and from the idol worshipers, much abuse. But if you persevere and lead a righteous life—that indeed is a mark of great determination.

187 God received a pledge from those who were given the Scripture: "You shall proclaim it to the people, and not conceal it." But they disregarded it behind their backs, and exchanged it for a small price. What a miserable exchange they made.

188 Do not think that those who rejoice in what they have done, and love to be praised for what they have not done—do not think they can evade the punishment. They will have a painful punishment.

189 To God belongs the sovereignty of the heavens and the earth. God has power over all things.

190 In the creation of the heavens and the earth, and in the alternation of night and day, are signs for people of understanding.

191 Those who remember God while standing, and sitting, and on their sides; and they reflect upon the creation of the heavens and the earth: "Our Lord, You did not create this in vain, glory to You, so protect us from the punishment of the Fire."

192 "Our Lord, whomever You commit to the Fire, You have disgraced. The wrongdoers will have no helpers."

193 "Our Lord, we have heard a caller calling to the faith: 'Believe in your Lord,' and we have believed. Our Lord! Forgive us our sins, and remit our misdeeds, and make us die in the company of the virtuous."

194 "Our Lord, and give us what You have promised us through Your messengers, and do not disgrace us on the Day of Resurrection. Surely You never break a promise."

195 And so their Lord answered them: "I will not waste the work of any worker among you, whether male or female. You are one of another. For those who emigrated, and were expelled from their homes, and were persecuted because of Me, and fought and were killed—I will remit for them their sins, and will admit them into gardens beneath which rivers flow—a reward from God. With God is the ultimate reward."

196 Do not be impressed by the disbelievers' movements in the land.

197 A brief enjoyment, then their abode is Hell. What a miserable resort.

198 As for those who feared their Lord: for them will be gardens beneath which rivers flow, wherein they will abide forever—hospitality from God. What God possesses is best for the just.

199 Among the People of the Scripture are those who believe in God, and in what was revealed to you, and in what was revealed to them. They are humble before God, and they do not sell God's revelations for a cheap price. These will have their reward with their Lord. God is swift in reckoning.

200 O you who believe! Be patient, and advocate patience, and be united, and revere God, so that you may thrive.

Joseph (Yusuf)

In the name of God, the Gracious, the Merciful.

1 Alif, Lam, Ra. These are the Verses of the Clear Book.

2 We have revealed it an Arabic Quran, so that you may understand.

3 We narrate to you the most accurate history, by revealing to you this Quran. Although, prior to it, you were of the unaware.

4 When Joseph said to his father, "O my father, I saw eleven planets, and the sun, and the moon; I saw them bowing down to me."

5 He said, "O my son, do not relate your vision to your brothers, lest they plot and scheme against you. Satan is man's sworn enemy.

6 And thus your Lord will choose you, and will teach you the interpretation of events, and will complete His blessing upon you and upon the family of Jacob, as He has completed it before upon your forefathers Abraham and Isaac. Your Lord is Knowing and Wise.

7 In Joseph and his brothers are lessons for the seekers.

8 When they said, "Joseph and his brother are dearer to our father than we are, although we are a whole group. Our father is obviously in the wrong.

9 "Kill Joseph, or throw him somewhere in the land, and your father's attention will be yours. Afterwards, you will be decent people."

10 One of them said, "Do not kill Joseph, but throw him into the bottom of the well; some caravan may pick him up—if you must do something."

11 They said, "Father, why do you not trust us with Joseph, although we care for him?"

12 "Send him with us tomorrow, that he may roam and play; we will take care of him."

13 He said, "It worries me that you would take him away. And I fear the wolf may eat him while you are careless of him."

14 They said, "If the wolf ate him, and we are many, we would be good for nothing."

15 So they went away with him, and agreed to put him at the bottom of the well. And We inspired him, "You will inform them of this deed of theirs when they are unaware."

16 And they came to their father in the evening weeping.

17 They said, "O father, we went off racing one another, and left Joseph by our belongings; and the wolf ate him. But you will not believe us, even though we are being truthful."

18 And they brought his shirt, with fake blood on it. He said, "Your souls enticed you to do something. But patience is beautiful, and God is my Help against what you describe."

19 A caravan passed by, and they sent their water-carrier. He lowered his bucket, and said, "Good news. Here is a boy." And they hid him as merchandise. But God was aware of what they did.

20 And they sold him for a cheap price—a few coins—they considered him to be of little value.

21 The Egyptian who bought him said to his wife, "Take good care of him; he may be useful to us, or we may adopt him as a son." We thus established Joseph in the land, to teach him the interpretation of events. God has control over His affairs, but most people do not know.

22 When he reached his maturity, We gave him wisdom and knowledge. We thus reward the righteous.

23 She in whose house he was living tried to seduce him. She shut the doors, and said, "I am yours." He said, "God forbid! He is my Lord. He has given me a good home. Sinners never succeed."

24 She desired him, and he desired her, had he not seen the proof of his Lord. It was thus that We diverted evil and indecency away from him. He was one of Our loyal servants.

25 As they raced towards the door, she tore his shirt from behind. At the door, they ran into her husband. She said, "What is the penalty for him who desired to dishonor your wife, except imprisonment or a painful punishment?"

26 He said, "It was she who tried to seduce me." A witness from her household suggested: "If his shirt is torn from the front: then she has told the truth, and he is the liar.

27 But if his shirt is torn from the back: then she has lied, and he is the truthful."

28 And when he saw that his shirt was torn from the back, he said, "This is a woman's scheme. Your scheming is serious indeed."

29 "Joseph, turn away from this. And you, woman, ask forgiveness for your sin; you are indeed in the wrong."

30 Some ladies in the city said, "The governor's wife is trying to seduce her servant. She is deeply in love with him. We see she has gone astray."

31 And when she heard of their gossip, she invited them, and prepared for them a banquet, and she gave each one of them a knife. She said, "Come out before them." And when they saw him, they marveled at him, and cut their hands. They said, "Good God, this is not a human, this must be a precious angel."

32 She said, "Here he is, the one you blamed me for. I did try to seduce him, but he resisted. But if he does not do what I tell him to do, he will be imprisoned, and will be one of the despised."

33 He said, "My Lord, prison is more desirable to me than what they call me to. Unless You turn their scheming away from me, I may yield to them, and become one of the ignorant."

34 Thereupon his Lord answered him, and diverted their scheming away from him. He is the Hearer, the Knower.

35 Then it occurred to them, after they had seen the signs, to imprison him for a while.

36 Two youth entered the prison with him. One of them said, "I see myself pressing wine." The other said, "I see myself carrying bread on my head, from which the birds are eating. Tell us their interpretation—we see that you are one of the righteous."

37 He said, "No food is served to you, but I have informed you about it before you have received it. That is some of what my Lord has taught me. I have forsaken the tradition of people who do not believe in God; and regarding the Hereafter, they are deniers."

38 "And I have followed the faith of my forefathers, Abraham, and Isaac, and Jacob. It is not for us to associate anything with God. This is by virtue of God's grace upon us and upon the people, but most people do not give thanks.

39 "O My fellow inmates, are diverse lords better, or God, the One, the Supreme?"

40 "You do not worship, besides Him, except names you have named, you and your ancestors, for which God has sent down no authority. Judgment belongs to none but God. He has commanded that you worship none but Him. This is the right religion, but most people do not know.

41 "O my fellow inmates! One of you will serve his master wine; while the other will be crucified, and the birds will eat from his head. Thus the matter you are inquiring about is settled."

42 And he said to the one he thought would be released, "Mention me to your master." But Satan caused him to forget mentioning him to his master, so he remained in prison for several years.

43 The king said, "I see seven fat cows being eaten by seven lean ones, and seven green spikes, and others dried up. O elders, explain to me my vision, if you are able to interpret visions."

44 They said, "Jumbles of dreams, and we know nothing of the interpretation of dreams."

45 The one who was released said, having remembered after a time, "I will inform you of its interpretation, so send me out."

46 "Joseph, O man of truth, inform us concerning seven fat cows being eaten by seven lean ones, and seven green spikes, and others dried up, so that I may return to the people, so that they may know."

47 He said, "You will farm for seven consecutive years. But whatever you harvest, leave it in its spikes, except for the little that you eat."

48 Then after that will come seven difficult ones, which will consume what you have stored for them, except for the little that you have preserved.

49 Then after that will come a year that brings relief to the people, and during which they will press.

50 The king said, "Bring him to me." And when the envoy came to him, he said, "Go back to your master, and ask him about the intentions of the women who cut their hands; my Lord is well aware of their schemes."

51 He said, "What was the matter with you, women, when you tried to seduce Joseph?" They said, "God forbid! We knew of no evil committed by him." The governor's wife then said, "Now the truth is out. It was I who tried to seduce him, and he is telling the truth."

52 "This is that he may know that I did not betray him in secret, and that God does not guide the scheming of the betrayers."

53 "Yet I do not claim to be innocent. The soul commands evil, except those on whom my Lord has mercy. Truly my Lord is Forgiving and Merciful."

54 The king said, "Bring him to me, and I will reserve him for myself." And when he spoke to him, he said, "This day you are with us established and secure."

55 He said, "Put me in charge of the storehouses of the land; I am honest and knowledgeable."

56 And thus We established Joseph in the land, to live therein wherever he wished. We touch with Our mercy whomever We will, and We never waste the reward of the righteous.

57 But the reward of the Hereafter is better for those who believe and observed piety.

58 And Joseph's brothers came, and entered into his presence. He recognized them, but they did not recognize him.

59 When he provided them with their provisions, he said, "Bring me a brother of yours from your father. Do you not see that I fill up the measure, and I am the best of hosts?"

60 "But if you do not bring him to me, you will have no measure from me, and you will not come near me."

61 They said, "We will solicit him from his father. We will surely do."

62 He said to his servants, "Put their goods in their saddlebags; perhaps they will recognize them when they return to their families, and maybe they will come back."

63 When they returned to their father, they said, "O father, we were denied measure, but send our brother with us, and we will obtain measure. We will take care of him."

64 He said, "Shall I trust you with him, as I trusted you with his brother before? God is the Best Guardian, and He is the Most Merciful of the merciful."

65 And when they opened their baggage, they found that their goods were returned to them. They said, "Father, what more do we want? Here are our goods, returned to us. We will provide for our family, and protect our brother, and have an additional camel-load. This is easy commerce."

66 He said, "I will not send him with you, unless you give me a pledge before God that you will bring him back to me, unless you get trapped." And when they gave him their pledge, he said, "God is witness to what we say."

67 And he said, "O my sons, do not enter by one gate, but enter by different gates. I cannot avail you anything against God. The decision rests only with God. On Him I rely, and on Him let the reliant rely."

68 And when they entered as their father had instructed them, it did not avail them anything against God; it was just a need in the soul of Jacob, which he carried out. He was a person of knowledge inasmuch as We had taught him, but most people do not know.

69 And when they entered into the presence of Joseph, he embraced his brother, and said, "I am your brother; do not be saddened by what they used to do."

70 Then, when he provided them with their provisions, he placed the drinking-cup in his brother's saddlebag. Then an announcer called out, "O people of the caravan, you are thieves."

71 They said, as they came towards them, "What are you missing?"

72 They said, "We are missing the king's goblet. Whoever brings it will have a camel-load; and I personally guarantee it."

73 They said, "By God, you know we did not come to cause trouble in the land, and we are not thieves."

74 They said, "What shall be his punishment, if you are lying?"

75 They said, "His punishment, if it is found in his bag: he will belong to you. Thus we penalize the guilty."

76 So he began with their bags, before his brother's bag. Then he pulled it out of his brother's bag. Thus We devised a plan for Joseph; he could not have detained his brother under the king's law, unless God so willed. We elevate by degrees whomever We will; and above every person of knowledge, there is one more learned.

77 They said, "If he has stolen, a brother of his has stolen before." But Joseph kept it to himself, and did not reveal it to them. He said, "You are in a worse situation, and God is Aware of what you allege."

78 They said, "O noble prince, he has a father, a very old man, so take one of us in his place. We see that you are a good person."

79 He said, "God forbid that we should arrest anyone except him in whose possession we found our property; for then we would be unjust."

80 And when they despaired of him, they conferred privately. Their eldest said, "Don't you know that your father received a pledge from you before God, and in the past you failed with regard to Joseph? I will not leave this land until my father permits me, or God decides for me; for He is the Best of Deciders."

81 "Go back to your father, and say, 'Our father, your son has stolen. We testify only to what we know, and we could not have prevented the unforeseen.'"

82 "Ask the town where we were, and the caravan in which we came. We are being truthful."

83 He said, "Rather, your souls have contrived something for you. Patience is a virtue. Perhaps God will bring them all back to me. He is the Knowing, the Wise."

84 Then he turned away from them, and said, "O my bitterness for Joseph." And his eyes turned white from sorrow, and he became depressed.

85 They said, "By God, you will not stop remembering Joseph, until you have ruined your health, or you have passed away."

86 He said, "I only complain of my grief and sorrow to God, and I know from God what you do not know."

87 "O my sons, go and inquire about Joseph and his brother, and do not despair of God's comfort. None despairs of God's comfort except the disbelieving people."

88 Then, when they entered into his presence, they said, "Mighty governor, adversity has befallen us, and our family. We have brought scant merchandise. But give us full measure, and be charitable towards us—God rewards the charitable."

89 He said, "Do you realize what you did with Joseph and his brother, in your ignorance?"

90 They said, "Is that you, Joseph?" He said, "I am Joseph, and this is my brother. God has been gracious to us. He who practices piety and patience—God never fails to reward the righteous."

91 They said, "By God, God has preferred you over us. We were definitely in the wrong."

92 He said, "There is no blame upon you today. God will forgive you. He is the Most Merciful of the merciful."

93 "Take this shirt of mine, and lay it over my father's face, and he will recover his sight. And bring your whole family to me."

94 As the caravan set out, their father said, "I sense the presence of Joseph, though you may think I am senile."

95 They said, "By God, you are still in your old confusion."

96 Then, when the bearer of good news arrived, he laid it over his face, and he regained his sight. He said, "Did I not say to you that I know from God what you do not know?"

97 They said, "Father, pray for the forgiveness of our sins; we were indeed at fault."

98 He said, "I will ask my Lord to forgive you. He is the Forgiver, the Most Merciful."

99 Then, when they entered into the presence of Joseph, he embraced his parents, and said, "Enter Egypt, God willing, safe and secure."

100 And he elevated his parents on the throne, and they fell prostrate before him. He said, "Father, this is the fulfillment of my vision of long ago. My Lord has made it come true. He has blessed me, when he released me from prison, and brought you out of the wilderness, after the devil had sown conflict between me and my brothers. My Lord is Most Kind towards whomever He wills. He is the All-knowing, the Most Wise."

101 "My Lord, You have given me some authority, and taught me some interpretation of events. Initiator of the heavens and the earth; You are my Protector in this life and in the Hereafter. Receive my soul in submission, and unite me with the righteous."

102 This is news from the past that We reveal to you. You were not present with them when they plotted and agreed on a plan.

103 But most people, for all your eagerness, are not believers.

104 You ask them no wage for it. It is only a reminder for all mankind.

105 How many a sign in the heavens and the earth do they pass by, paying no attention to them?

106 And most of them do not believe in God unless they associate others.

107 Do they feel secure that a covering of God's punishment will not come upon them, or that the Hour will not come upon them suddenly, while they are unaware?

108 Say, "This is my way; I invite to God, based on clear knowledge—I and whoever follows me. Glory be to God; and I am not of the polytheists."

109 We did not send before you except men, whom We inspired, from the people of the towns. Have they not roamed the earth and seen the consequences for those before them? The Home of the Hereafter is better for those who are righteous. Do you not understand?

110 Until, when the messengers have despaired, and thought that they were rejected, Our help came to them. We save whomever We will, and Our severity is not averted from the guilty people.

111 In their stories is a lesson for those who possess intelligence. This is not a fabricated tale, but a confirmation of what came before it, and a detailed explanation of all things, and guidance, and mercy for people who believe.

Abraham (Ibrahim)

In the name of God, the Gracious, the Merciful.

1 Alif, Lam, Ra. A Scripture that We revealed to you, that you may bring humanity from darkness to light—with the permission of their Lord—to the path of the Almighty, the Praiseworthy.

2 God—to whom belongs what is in the heavens and the earth. And woe to the disbelievers from a severe torment.

3 Those who prefer the present life to the Hereafter, and repel from the path of God, and seek to make it crooked—these are far astray.

4 We never sent any messenger except in the language of his people, to make things clear for them. God leads astray whom He wills, and guides whom He wills. He is the Mighty, the Wise.

5 We sent Moses with Our signs: "Bring your people out of darkness into light, and remind them of the Days of God." In that are signs for every patient and thankful person."

6 Moses said to his people, "Remember God's blessings upon you, as He delivered you from the people of Pharaoh, who inflicted on you terrible suffering, slaughtering your sons while sparing your daughters. In that was a serious trial from your Lord."

7 And when your Lord proclaimed: "If you give thanks, I will grant you increase; but if you are ungrateful, My punishment is severe."

8 And Moses said, "Even if you are ungrateful, together with everyone on earth—God is in no need, Worthy of Praise."

9 Has not the story reached you, of those before you, the people of Noah, and Aad, and Thamood—and those after them? None knows them except God.

Their messengers came to them with the clear proofs, but they tried to silence them, and said, "We reject what you are sent with, and we are in serious doubt regarding what you are calling us to."

10 Their messengers said, "Is there any doubt about God, Maker of the heavens and the earth? He calls you to forgive you your sins, and to defer you until a stated term." They said, "You are only humans like us; you want to turn us away from what our ancestors worshiped; so bring us a clear proof."

11 Their messengers said to them, "We are only humans like you, but God favors whomever He wills from among His servants. We cannot possibly show you any proof, except by leave of God. In God let the faithful put their trust."

12 "And why should we not trust in God, when He has guided us in our ways? We will persevere in the face of your persecution. And upon God the reliant should rely."

13 Those who disbelieved said to their messengers, "We will expel you from our land, unless you return to our religion." And their Lord inspired them: "We will destroy the wrongdoers."

14 "And We will settle you in the land after them. That is for him who fears My Majesty, and fears My threats."

15 And they prayed for victory, and every stubborn tyrant came to disappointment.

16 Beyond him lies Hell, and he will be given to drink putrid water.

17 He will guzzle it, but he will not swallow it. Death will come at him from every direction, but he will not die. And beyond this is relentless suffering.

18 The likeness of those who disbelieve in their Lord: their works are like ashes, in a fierce wind, on a stormy day. They have no control over anything they have earned. That is the utmost misguidance.

19 Do you not see that God created the heavens and the earth with truth? If He wills, He can do away with you, and bring a new creation.

20 And that is not difficult for God.

21 They will emerge before God, altogether. The weak will say to those who were proud, "We were your followers, can you protect us at all against God's punishment?" They will say, "Had God guided us, we would have guided you. It is the same for us; whether we mourn, or are patient; there is no asylum for us."

22 And Satan will say, when the issue is settled, "God has promised you the promise of truth, and I promised you, but I failed you. I had no authority over you, except that I called you, and you answered me. So do not blame me, but blame yourselves. I cannot come to your aid, nor can you come to my aid. I reject your associating with me in the past. The wrongdoers will have a torment most painful."

23 But those who believed and did good deeds will be admitted into gardens beneath which rivers flow, to remain therein forever, by leave of their Lord. Their greeting therein will be: "Peace."

24 Do you not see how God presents a parable? A good word is like a good tree—its root is firm, and its branches are in the sky.

25 It yields its fruits every season by the will of its Lord. God presents the parables to the people, so that they may reflect.

26 And the parable of a bad word is that of a bad tree—it is uprooted from the ground; it has no stability.

27 God gives firmness to those who believe, with the firm word, in this life, and in the Hereafter. And God leads the wicked astray. God does whatever He wills.

28 Have you not seen those who exchanged the blessing of God with blasphemy, and landed their people into the house of perdition?

29 Hell—they will roast in it. What a miserable settlement.

30 And they set up rivals to God, in order to lead away from His path. Say, "Enjoy yourselves; your destination is the Fire."

31 Tell My servants who have believed to perform the prayers, and to give from what We have given them, secretly and publicly, before a Day comes in which there is neither trading nor friendship.

32 God is He Who created the heavens and the earth, and sends down water from the sky, and with it produces fruits for your sustenance. And He committed the ships to your service, sailing through the sea by His command, and He committed the rivers to your service.

33 And He committed the sun and the moon to your service, both continuously pursuing their courses, and He committed the night and the day to your service.

34 And He has given you something of all what you asked. And if you were to count God's blessings, you would not be able to enumerate them. The human being is unfair and ungrateful.

35 Recall that Abraham said, "O my Lord, make this land peaceful, and keep me and my sons from worshiping idols."

36 "My Lord, they have led many people astray. Whoever follows me belongs with me; and whoever disobeys me—You are Forgiving and Merciful.

37 "Our Lord, I have settled some of my offspring in a valley of no vegetation, by Your Sacred House, our Lord, so that they may perform the prayers. So make the hearts of some people incline towards them, and provide them with fruits, that they may be thankful."

38 "Our Lord, You know what we conceal and what we reveal. And nothing is hidden from God, on earth or in the heaven."

39 "Praise be to God, Who has given me, in my old age, Ishmael and Isaac. My Lord is the Hearer of Prayers."

40 "My Lord, make me one who performs the prayer, and from my offspring. Our Lord, accept my supplication."

41 "Our Lord, forgive me, and my parents, and the believers, on the Day the Reckoning takes place."

42 Do not ever think that God is unaware of what the wrongdoers do. He only defers them until a Day when the sights stare.

43 Their necks outstretched, their heads upraised, their gaze unblinking, their hearts void.

44 And warn mankind of the Day when the punishment will come upon them, and the wicked will say, "Our Lord, defer us for a little while, and we will answer Your call and follow the messengers." Did you not swear before that there will be no passing away for you?

45 And you inhabited the homes of those who wronged themselves, and it became clear to you how We dealt with them, and We cited for you the examples.

46 They planned their plans, but their plans are known to God, even if their plans can eliminate mountains.

47 Do not ever think that God will break His promise to His messengers. God is Strong, Able to Avenge.

48 On the Day when the earth is changed into another earth, and the heavens, and they will emerge before God, the One, the Irresistible.

49 On that Day, you will see the sinners bound together in chains.

50 Their garments made of tar, and the Fire covering their faces.

51 That God may repay each soul according to what it has earned. God is Quick in reckoning.

52 This is a proclamation for mankind, that they may be warned thereby, and know that He is One God, and that people of understanding may remember.

The Bee (an-Nahl)

In the name of God, the Gracious, the Merciful.

1 The command of God has come, so do not rush it. Glory be to Him; exalted above what they associate.

2 He sends down the angels with the Spirit by His command, upon whom He wills of His servants: "Give warning that there is no god but Me, and fear Me."

3 He created the heavens and the earth with justice. He is exalted above the associations they attribute.

4 He created the human being from a drop of fluid, yet he becomes an open adversary.

5 And the livestock—He created them for you. In them are warmth and benefits for you, and of them you eat.

6 And there is beauty in them for you, when you bring them home, and when you drive them to pasture.

7 And they carry your loads to territory you could not have reached without great hardship. Your Lord is Clement and Merciful.

8 And the horses, and the mules, and the donkeys—for you to ride, and for luxury. And He creates what you do not know.

9 It is for God to point out the paths, but some of them are flawed. Had He willed, He could have guided you all.

10 It is He Who sends down for you from the sky water. From it is drink, and with it grows vegetation for grazing.

11 And He produces for you grains with it, and olives, and date-palms, and grapes, and all kinds of fruits. Surely in that is a sign for people who think.

12 And He regulated for you the night and the day; and the sun, and the moon, and the stars are disposed by His command. Surely in that are signs for people who ponder.

13 And whatsoever He created for you on earth is of diverse colors. Surely in that is a sign for people who are mindful.

14 And it is He who made the sea to serve you, that you may eat from it tender meat, and extract from it ornaments that you wear. And you see the ships plowing through it, as you seek His bounties, so that you may give thanks.

15 And he cast mountains on the earth, lest it shifts with you; and rivers, and roads, so that you may be guided.

16 And landmarks. And by the stars they guide themselves.

17 Is He who creates like him who does not create? Will you not take a lesson?

18 And if you tried to enumerate the favors of God, you will not be able to count them. God is Forgiving and Merciful.

19 And God knows what you hide and what you disclose.

20 Those they invoke besides God create nothing, but are themselves created.

21 They are dead, not alive; and they do not know when they will be resurrected.

22 Your God is one God. As for those who do not believe in the Hereafter, their hearts are in denial, and they are arrogant.

23 Without a doubt, God knows what they conceal and what they reveal. He does not like the arrogant.

24 And when it is said to them, "What has your Lord sent down?" They say, "Legends of the ancients."

25 So let them carry their loads complete on the Day of Resurrection, and some of the loads of those they misguided without knowledge. Evil is what they carry.

26 Those before them also schemed, but God took their structures from the foundations, and the roof caved in on them. The punishment came at them from where they did not perceive.

27 Then, on the Day of Resurrection, He will disgrace them, and say, "Where are My associates for whose sake you used to dispute?" Those who were given knowledge will say, "Today shame and misery are upon the disbelievers."

28 Those wronging their souls while the angels are taking them away—they will propose peace: "We did no wrong." Yes you did. God is aware of what you used to do."

29 Enter the gates of Hell, to dwell therein forever. Miserable is the residence of the arrogant.

30 And it will be said to those who maintained piety, "What has your Lord revealed?" They will say, "Goodness." To those who do good in this world is goodness, and the Home of the Hereafter is even better. How wonderful is the residence of the pious.

31 The Gardens of Perpetuity, which they will enter, beneath which rivers flow, where they will have whatever they desire. Thus God rewards the pious.

32 Those who are in a wholesome state when the angels take them—will say, "Peace be upon you; enter Paradise, for what you used to do."

33 Are they but waiting for the angels to come to them, or for the command of your Lord to arrive? Those before them did likewise. God did not wrong them, but they used to wrong their own souls.

34 So the evils of their deeds assailed them, and what they used to ridicule engulfed them.

35 The idolaters say, "Had God willed, we would not have worshiped anything besides Him, neither us, nor our ancestors, nor would we have prohibited anything besides His prohibitions." Those before them did likewise. Are the messengers responsible for anything but clear communication?

36 To every community We sent a messenger: "Worship God, and avoid idolatry." Some of them God guided, while others deserved misguidance. So travel through the earth, and see what the fate of the deniers was.

37 Even though you may be concerned about their guidance, God does not guide those who misguide. And they will have no saviors.

38 And they swear by God with their most solemn oaths, "God will not resurrect anyone who dies." Yes indeed, it is a promise binding on Him, but most people do not know.

39 To clarify for them what they differed about, and for the faithless to know that they were liars.

40 When We intend for something to happen, We say to it, "Be," and it becomes.

41 Those who emigrate for God's sake after being persecuted, We will settle them in a good place in this world; but the reward of the Hereafter is greater, if they only knew.

42 Those who endure patiently, and in their Lord they put their trust.

43 We did not send before you except men whom We inspired. So ask the people of knowledge, if you do not know.

44 With the clarifications and the scriptures. And We revealed to you the Reminder, that you may clarify to the people what was revealed to them, and that they may reflect.

45 Do those who scheme evils feel secure that God will not cause the earth to cave in with them, or that the punishment will not come upon them from where they do not perceive?

46 Or that He will not seize them during their activities? And they will not be able to prevent it.

47 Or that He will not seize them while in dread? Your Lord is Gentle and Merciful.

48 Have they not observed what God has created? Their shadows revolve from the right and the left, bowing to God as they shrink away.

49 To God bows down everything in the heavens and everything on earth—every living creature, and the angels, and without being proud.

50 They fear their Lord above them, and they do what they are commanded.

51 God has said: "Do not take two gods; He is only One God; so fear only Me."

52 To Him belongs everything in the heavens and the earth; and to Him obedience is due always. Do you, then, fear anyone other than God?

53 Whatever blessing you have is from God. And when harm touches you, it is to Him that you groan.

54 But when He lifts the harm from you, some of you associate others with their Lord.

55 To show ingratitude for what We have given them. Enjoy yourselves. You will soon know.

56 And they allocate, to something they do not know, a share of what We have provided for them. By God, you will be questioned about what you have been inventing.

57 And they attribute to God daughters—exalted is He—and for themselves what they desire.

58 And when one of them is given news of a female infant, his face darkens, and he chokes with grief.

59 He hides from the people because of the bad news given to him. Shall he keep it in humiliation, or bury it in the dust? Evil is the decision they make.

60 Those who do not believe in the Hereafter set a bad example, while God sets the Highest Example. He is the Mighty, the Wise.

61 If God were to hold mankind for their injustices, He would not leave upon it a single creature, but He postpones them until an appointed time. Then, when their time arrives, they will not delay it by one hour, nor will they advance it.

62 And they attribute to God what they themselves dislike, while their tongues utter the lie that theirs is the goodness. Without a doubt, for them is the Fire, and they will be neglected.

63 By God, We sent messengers to communities before you, but Satan made their deeds appear alluring to them. He is their master today, and they will have a painful punishment.

64 We revealed to you the Scripture only to clarify for them what they differ about, and guidance and mercy for people who believe.

65 God sends down water from the sky, with which He revives the earth after its death. In this is a sign for people who listen.

66 And there is a lesson for you in cattle: We give you a drink from their bellies, from between waste and blood, pure milk, refreshing to the drinkers.

67 And from the fruits of date-palms and grapevines, you derive sugar and wholesome food. In this is a sign for people who understand.

68 And your Lord inspired the bee: "Set up hives in the mountains, and in the trees, and in what they construct."

69 Then eat of all the fruits, and go along the pathways of your Lord, with precision. From their bellies emerges a fluid of diverse colors, containing healing for the people. Surely in this is a sign for people who reflect.

70 God created you; then He takes you away. Some of you will be brought back to the worst age, so that he will no longer know anything, after having acquired knowledge. God is Omniscient and Omnipotent.

71 God has favored some of you over others in livelihood. Those who are favored would not give their properties to their servants, to the extent of making them partners in it. Will they then renounce God's blessings?

72 God has given you mates from among yourselves; and has produced for you, from your mates, children and grandchildren; and has provided you with good things. Will they then believe in falsehood, and refuse God's favors?

73 And yet they serve besides God what possesses no provisions for them in the heavens, nor on earth, nor are they capable.

74 So do not cite the examples for God. God knows, and you do not know.

75 God cites the example of a bonded slave, who has no power over anything; and someone to whom We have given plentiful provision, from which he gives secretly and openly. Are they equal in comparison? All praise belongs to God, but most of them do not know.

76 And God cites the example of two men: one of them dumb, unable to do anything, and is a burden on his master; whichever way he directs him, he achieves nothing good. Is he equal to him who commands justice, and is on a straight path?

77 To God belongs the unseen of the heavens and the earth. The coming of the Hour is only as the twinkling of the eye, or even nearer. God has power over everything.

78 God brought you out of your mothers' wombs, not knowing anything; and He gave you the hearing, and the eyesight, and the brains; that you may give thanks.

79 Have they not seen the birds, flying in the midst of the sky? None sustains them except God. In this are signs for people who believe.

80 And God has given you in your homes habitats for you, and has provided for you out of the hides of livestock portable homes for you, so you can use them when you travel, and when you camp; and from their wool, and fur, and hair, furnishings and comfort for a while.

81 And God has made for you shade out of what He has created, and has given you resorts in the mountains, and has given you garments to protect you from the heat, and garments to protect you from your violence. Thus He completes His blessings upon you, so that you may submit.

82 But if they turn away, your only duty is clear communication.

83 They recognize God's blessing, but then deny it, as most of them are ungrateful.

84 On the Day when We raise up a witness from every community—those who disbelieved will not be permitted, nor will they be excused.

85 When those who did wrong see the punishment, it will not be lightened for them, nor will they be reprieved.

86 And when the idolaters see their associates, they will say, "Our Lord, these are our associates whom we used to invoke besides You." They will strike back at them with the saying, "Surely you are liars."

87 On that Day they will offer their submission to God, and what they had invented will abandon them.

88 Those who disbelieve and obstruct from God's path—We will add punishment to their punishment, on account of the mischief they used to make.

89 On the Day when We raise in every community a witness against them, from among them, and bring you as a witness against these. We have revealed to you the Book, as an explanation of all things, and guidance, and mercy and good news for those who submit.

90 God commands justice, and goodness, and generosity towards relatives. And He forbids immorality, and injustice, and oppression. He advises you, so that you may take heed.

91 Fulfill God's covenant when you make a covenant, and do not break your oaths after ratifying them. You have made God your guarantor, and God knows what you do.

92 And do not be like her who unravels her yarn, breaking it into pieces, after she has spun it strongly. Nor use your oaths as means of deception among you, because one community is more prosperous than another. God is testing you thereby. On the Day of Resurrection, He will make clear to you everything you had disputed about.

93 Had God willed, He would have made you one congregation, but He leaves astray whom He wills, and He guides whom He wills. And you will surely be questioned about what you used to do.

94 And do not use your oaths to deceive one another, so that a foot may not slip after being firm, and you taste misery because you hindered from God's path, and incur a terrible torment.

95 And do not exchange God's covenant for a small price. What is with God is better for you, if you only knew.

96 What you have runs out, but what is with God remains. We will reward those who are patient according to the best of their deeds.

97 Whoever works righteousness, whether male or female, while being a believer, We will grant him a good life—and We will reward them according to the best of what they used to do.

98 When you read the Quran, seek refuge with God from Satan the outcast.

99 He has no authority over those who believe and trust in their Lord.

100 His authority is only over those who follow him, and those who associate others with Him.

101 When We substitute a verse in place of another verse—and God knows best what He reveals—they say, "You are an impostor." But most of them do not know.

102 Say, "The Holy Spirit has brought it down from your Lord, truthfully, in order to stabilize those who believe, and as guidance and good news for those who submit."

103 We are well aware that they say, "It is a human being who is teaching him." But the tongue of him they allude to is foreign, while this is a clear Arabic tongue.

104 Those who do not believe in God's revelations—God will not guide them, and for them is a painful punishment.

105 It is those who do not believe in God's revelations who fabricate falsehood. These are the liars.

106 Whoever renounces faith in God after having believed—except for someone who is compelled, while his heart rests securely in faith—but whoever willingly opens up his heart to disbelief—upon them falls wrath from God, and for them is a tremendous torment.

107 That is because they have preferred the worldly life to the Hereafter, and because God does not guide the people who refuse.

108 It is they whom God has sealed their hearts, and their hearing, and their sight. It is they who are the heedless.

109 There is no doubt that in the Hereafter they will be the losers.

110 But then your Lord—for those who emigrated after being persecuted, then struggled and persevered—your Lord thereafter is Forgiving and Merciful.

111 On the Day when every soul will come pleading for itself, and every soul will be paid in full for what it has done, and they will not be wronged.

112 And God cites the example of a town that was secure and peaceful, with its livelihood coming to it abundantly from every direction. But then it turned unappreciative of God's blessings, so God made it taste the robe of hunger and fear, because of what they used to craft.

113 A messenger from among them had come to them, but they denounced him, so the punishment seized them in the midst of their wrongdoing.

114 Eat of the lawful and good things God has provided for you, and be thankful for God's blessings, if it is Him that you serve.

115 He has forbidden you carrion, and blood, and the flesh of swine, and anything consecrated to other than God. But if anyone is compelled by necessity, without being deliberate or malicious, then God is Forgiving and Merciful.

116 And do not say of falsehood asserted by your tongues, "This is lawful, and this is unlawful," in order to invent lies and attribute them to God. Those who invent lies and attribute them to God will not succeed.

117 A brief enjoyment—then they will have a painful punishment.

118 For those who are Jews, We have prohibited what We related to you before. We did not wrong them, but they used to wrong their own selves.

119 But towards those who do wrongs in ignorance, and then repent afterwards and reform, your Lord thereafter is Forgiving and Merciful.

120 Abraham was an exemplary leader, devoted to God, a monotheist, and was not of the polytheists.

121 Thankful for His blessings. He chose him, and guided him to a straight path.

122 And We gave him goodness in this world, and in the Hereafter he will be among the righteous.

123 Then We inspired you: "Follow the religion of Abraham, the Monotheist. He was not an idol-worshiper."

124 The Sabbath was decreed only for those who differed about it. Your Lord will judge between them on the Day of Resurrection regarding their differences.

125 Invite to the way of your Lord with wisdom and good advice, and debate with them in the most dignified manner. Your Lord is aware of those who stray from His path, and He is aware of those who are guided.

126 If you were to retaliate, retaliate to the same degree as the injury done to you. But if you resort to patience—it is better for the patient.

127 So be patient. Your patience is solely from God. And do not grieve over them, and do not be stressed by their schemes.

128 God is with those who are righteous and those who are virtuous.

The Night Journey (al-Isra')

In the name of God, the Gracious, the Merciful.

1 Glory to Him who journeyed His servant by night, from the Sacred Mosque, to the Farthest Mosque, whose precincts We have blessed, in order to show him of Our wonders. He is the Listener, the Beholder.

2 And We gave Moses the Scripture, and made it a guide for the Children of Israel: Take none for protector other than Me.

3 The descendants of those We carried with Noah. He was an appreciative servant.

4 And We conveyed to the Children of Israel in the Scripture: You will commit evil on earth twice, and you will rise to a great height.

5 When the first of the two promises came true, We sent against you servants of Ours, possessing great might, and they ransacked your homes. It was a promise fulfilled.

6 Then We gave you back your turn against them, and supplied you with wealth and children, and made you more numerous.

7 If you work righteousness, you work righteousness for yourselves; and if you commit evil, you do so against yourselves. Then, when the second promise comes true, they will make your faces filled with sorrow, and enter the Temple as they entered it the first time, and utterly destroy all that falls into their power.

8 Perhaps your Lord will have mercy on you. But if you revert, We will revert. We have made Hell a prison for the disbelievers.

9 This Quran guides to what is most upright; and it gives good news to the believers who do good deeds, that they will have a great reward.

10 And those who do not believe in the Hereafter—We have prepared for them a painful punishment.

11 The human being prays for evil as he prays for good. The human being is very hasty.

12 We have made the night and the day two wonders. We erased the wonder of the night, and made the wonder of the day revealing, that you may seek bounty from your Lord, and know the number of years, and the calculation. We have explained all things in detail.

13 For every person We have attached his fate to his neck. And on the Day of Resurrection, We will bring out for him a book which he will find spread open.

14 "Read your book; today there will be none but yourself to call you to account."

15 Whoever is guided—is guided for his own good. And whoever goes astray—goes astray to his detriment. No burdened soul carries the burdens of another, nor do We ever punish until We have sent a messenger.

16 When We decide to destroy a town, We command its affluent ones, they transgress in it, so the word becomes justified against it, and We destroy it completely.

17 How many generations have We destroyed after Noah? Your Lord is sufficient as Knower and Beholder of the sins of his servants.

18 Whoever desires the fleeting life, We expedite for him what We decide to give him, to whomever We desire. Then We consign him to Hell, where he will roast, condemned and defeated.

19 But whoever desires the Hereafter, and pursues it as it should be pursued, while he is a believer; these—their effort will be appreciated.

20 To all—these and those—We extend from the gifts of your Lord. The gifts of your Lord are not restricted.

21 See how We have favored some of them over others; yet the Hereafter is greater in ranks, and greater in favors.

22 Do not set up another god with God, lest you become condemned and damned.

23 Your Lord has commanded that you worship none but Him, and that you be good to your parents. If either of them or both of them reach old age with you, do not say to them a word of disrespect, nor scold them, but say to them kind words.

24 And lower to them the wing of humility, out of mercy, and say, "My Lord, have mercy on them, as they raised me when I was a child."

25 Your Lord knows best what is in your minds. If you are righteous—He is Forgiving to the obedient.

26 And give the relative his rights, and the poor, and the wayfarer, and do not squander wastefully.

27 The extravagant are brethren of the devils, and the devil is ever ungrateful to his Lord.

28 But if you turn away from them, seeking mercy from your Lord which you hope for, then say to them words of comfort.

29 And do not keep your hand tied to your neck, nor spread it out fully, lest you end up liable and regretful.

30 Your Lord expands the provision for whomever He wills, and restricts it. He is fully Informed, Observant of His servants.

31 And do not kill your children for fear of poverty. We provide for them, and for you. Killing them is a grave sin.

32 And do not come near adultery. It is immoral, and an evil way.

33 And do not kill the soul which God has made sacred, except in the course of justice. If someone is killed unjustly, We have given his next of kin certain authority. But he should not be excessive in killing, for he will be supported.

34 And do not go near the orphan's property, except with the best of intentions, until he has reached his maturity. And honor your pledge, because the pledge involves responsibility.

35 And give full measure when you measure, and weigh with accurate scales. That is fair, and the best determination.

36 And do not occupy yourself with what you have no knowledge of. The hearing, and the sight, and the brains—all these will be questioned.

37 And do not walk proudly on earth. You can neither pierce the earth, nor can you match the mountains in height.

38 The evil of all these is disliked by your Lord.

39 That is some of the wisdom your Lord has revealed to you. Do not set up with God another god, or else you will be thrown in Hell, rebuked and banished.

40 Has your Lord favored you with sons, while choosing for Himself daughters from among the angels? You are indeed saying a terrible thing.

41 We have explained in this Quran in various ways, that they may remember, but it only adds to their rebellion.

42 Say, "If there were other gods with Him, as they say, they would have sought a way to the Lord of the Throne."

43 Be He glorified. He is exalted, far above what they say.

44 Praising Him are the seven heavens, and the earth, and everyone in them. There is not a thing that does not glorify Him with praise, but you do not understand their praises. He is indeed Forbearing and Forgiving.

45 When you read the Quran, We place between you and those who do not believe in the Hereafter an invisible barrier.

46 And We drape veils over their hearts, preventing them from understanding it, and heaviness in their ears. And when you mention your Lord alone in the Quran, they turn their backs in aversion.

47 We know well what they listen to, when they listen to you, as they conspire, when the wrongdoers say, "You only follow a man bewitched."

48 Note what they compared you to. They are lost, and unable to find a way.

49 And they say, "When we have become bones and fragments, shall we really be resurrected as a new creation?"

50 Say, "Even if you become rocks or iron.

51 Or some substance, which, in your minds, is even harder." Then they will say, "Who will restore us?" Say, "The One who originated you the first time." Then they will nod their heads at you, and say, "When will it be?" Say, "Perhaps it will be soon."

52 On the Day when He calls you, you will respond with His praise, and you will realize that you stayed only a little.

53 Tell My servants to say what is best. Satan sows discord among them. Satan is to man an open enemy.

54 Your Lord knows you best. If He wills, He will have mercy on you; and if He wills, He will punish you. We did not send you as their advocate.

55 Your Lord knows well everyone in the heavens and the earth. We have given some prophets advantage over others; and to David We gave the Psalms.

56 Say, "Call upon those you claim besides Him. They have no power to relieve your adversity, nor can they change it."

57 Those they call upon are themselves seeking means of access to their Lord, vying to be nearer, and hoping for His mercy, and fearing His punishment. The punishment of your Lord is to be dreaded.

58 There is no city but We will destroy before the Day of Resurrection, or punish it with a severe punishment. This is inscribed in the Book.

59 Nothing prevents Us from sending miraculous signs, except that the ancients called them lies. We gave Thamood the she-camel, a visible sign, but they mistreated her. We do not send the signs except to instill reverence.

60 We said to you that your Lord encompasses humanity. We did not make the vision We showed you, except as a test for the people, and the tree cursed in the Quran. We frighten them, but that only increases their defiance.

61 When We said to the angels, "Bow down before Adam," they bowed down, except for Satan. He said, "Shall I bow down before someone You created from mud?"

62 He said, "Do You see this one whom You have honored more than me? If You reprieve me until the Day of Resurrection, I will bring his descendants under my sway, except for a few."

63 He said, "Begone! Whoever of them follows you—Hell is your reward, an ample reward."

64 "And entice whomever of them you can with your voice, and rally against them your cavalry and your infantry, and share with them in wealth and children, and make promises to them." But Satan promises them nothing but delusion.

65 "As for My devotees, you have no authority over them." Your Lord is an adequate Guardian.

66 Your Lord is He who propels for you the ships at sea, that you may seek of His bounty. He is towards you Most Merciful.

67 When harm afflicts you at sea, those you pray to vanish, except for Him. But when He saves you to land, you turn away. The human being is ever thankless.

68 Are you confident that He will not cause a track of land to cave in beneath you, or unleash a tornado against you, and then you find no protector?

69 Or are you confident that He will not return you to it once again, and unleash a hurricane against you, and drown you for your ingratitude? Then you will find no helper against Us.

70 We have honored the Children of Adam, and carried them on land and sea, and provided them with good things, and greatly favored them over many of those We created.

71 On the Day when We call every people with their leader. Whoever is given his record in his right hand—these will read their record, and they will not be wronged one bit.

72 But whoever is blind in this, he will be blind in the Hereafter, and further astray from the way.

73 They almost lured you away from what We have revealed to you, so that you would invent something else in Our name. In that case, they would have taken you for a friend.

74 Had We not given you stability, you might have inclined towards them a little.

75 Then We would have made you taste double in life, and double at death; then you would have found for yourself no helper against Us.

76 They almost provoked you, to expel you from the land. In that case, they would not have lasted after you, except briefly.

77 The tradition of the messengers We sent before you—you will find no change in Our rules.

78 Perform the prayer at the decline of the sun, until the darkness of the night; and the Quran at dawn. The Quran at dawn is witnessed.

79 And keep vigil with it during parts of the night, as an extra prayer. Perhaps your Lord will raise you to a laudable position.

80 And say, "My Lord, lead me in through an entry of truth, and lead me out through an exit of truth, and grant me from You a supporting power."

81 And say, "The truth has come, and falsehood has withered away; for falsehood is bound to wither away."

82 We send down in the Quran healing and mercy for the believers, but it increases the wrongdoers only in loss.

83 When We bless the human being, he turns away and distances himself. But when adversity touches him, he is in despair.

84 Say, "Each does according to his disposition. Your Lord knows best who is better guided in the way."

85 And they ask you about the Spirit. Say, "The Spirit belongs to the domain of my Lord; and you were given only little knowledge."

86 If We willed, We could take away what We revealed to you. Then you will find for yourself no protecting guardian against Us.

87 Except through a mercy from your Lord. His favors upon you have been great.

88 Say, "If mankind and jinn came together to produce the like of this Quran, they could never produce the like of it, even if they backed up one another."

89 We have displayed for mankind in this Quran every kind of similitude, but most people insist on denying the truth.

90 And they said, "We will not believe in you unless you make a spring burst from the ground for us.

91 Or you have a garden of palms and vines; then cause rivers to gush pouring through them.

92 Or make the sky fall on us in pieces, as you claim, or bring God and the angels before us.

93 Or you possess a house of gold. Or you ascend into the sky. Even then, we will not believe in your ascension, unless you bring down for us a book that we can read." Say, "Glory be to my Lord. Am I anything but a human messenger?"

94 Nothing prevented the people from believing, when guidance has come to them, except that they said, "Did God send a human messenger?"

95 Say, "If there were angels on earth, walking around in peace, We would have sent down to them from heaven an angel messenger."

96 Say, "God is enough witness between you and me. He is fully aware of His servants, and He sees them well."

97 Whomever God guides is the guided one. And whomever He leaves astray—for them you will find no protectors apart from Him. And We will gather them on the Day of Resurrection, on their faces, blind, dumb, and deaf. Their abode is Hell; whenever it abates, We intensify the blaze for them.

98 This is their repayment for having blasphemed against Our revelations, and having said, "Shall we, when we have become bones and fragments, be resurrected as a new creation?"

99 Do they not consider that God, Who created the heavens and the earth, is Able to create the likes of them? He has assigned for them a term, in which there is no doubt. But the wrongdoers persist in denying the truth.

100 Say, "If you possessed the treasuries of my Lord's mercy, you would have withheld them for fear of spending." The human being has always been stingy.

101 We gave Moses nine clear signs—ask the Children of Israel. When he went to them, Pharaoh said to him, "I think that you, Moses, are bewitched."

102 He said, "You know that none sent these down except the Lord of the heavens and the earth—eye openers; and I think that you, Pharaoh, are doomed."

103 He resolved to scare them off the land, but We drowned him, and those with him, altogether.

104 After him, We said to the Children of Israel, "Inhabit the land, and when the promise of the Hereafter arrives, We will bring you all together."

105 With the truth We sent it down, and with the truth it descended. We sent you only as a bearer of good news and a warner.

106 A Quran which We unfolded gradually, that you may recite to the people over time. And We revealed it in stages.

107 Say, "Believe in it, or do not believe." Those who were given knowledge before it, when it is recited to them, they fall to their chins, prostrating.

108 And they say, "Glory to our Lord. The promise of our Lord is fulfilled."

109 And they fall to their chins, weeping, and it adds to their humility.

110 Say, "Call Him God, or call Him the Most Merciful. Whichever name you use, to Him belong the Best Names." And be neither loud in your prayer, nor silent in it, but follow a course in between.

111 And say, "Praise be to God, who has not begotten a son, nor has He a partner in sovereignty, nor has He an ally out of weakness, and glorify Him constantly."

Mary (Maryam)

In the name of God, the Gracious, the Merciful.

1 Kaf, Ha, Ya, Ayn, Saad.

2 A mention of the mercy of your Lord towards His servant Zechariah.

3 When he called on his Lord, a call in seclusion.

4 He said, "My Lord, my bones have become feeble, and my hair is aflame with gray, and never, Lord, have I been disappointed in my prayer to you.

5 "And I fear for my dependents after me, and my wife is barren. So grant me, from Yourself, an heir.

6 To inherit me, and inherit from the House of Jacob, and make him, my Lord, pleasing."

7 "O Zechariah, We give you good news of a son, whose name is John, a name We have never given before."

8 He said, "My Lord, how can I have a son, when my wife is barren, and I have become decrepit with old age?"

9 He said, "It will be so, your Lord says, 'it is easy for me, and I created you before, when you were nothing.'"

10 He said, "My Lord, give me a sign." He said, "Your sign is that you will not speak to the people for three nights straight."

11 And he came out to his people, from the sanctuary, and signaled to them to praise morning and evening.

12 "O John, hold on to the Scripture firmly," and We gave him wisdom in his youth.

13 And tenderness from Us, and innocence. He was devout.

14 And kind to his parents; and he was not a disobedient tyrant.

15 And peace be upon him the day he was born, and the day he dies, and the Day he is raised alive.

16 And mention in the Scripture Mary, when she withdrew from her people to an eastern location.

17 She screened herself away from them, and We sent to her Our spirit, and He appeared to her as an immaculate human.

18 She said, "I take refuge from you in the Most Merciful, should you be righteous."

19 He said, "I am only the messenger of your Lord, to give you the gift of a pure son."

20 She said, "How can I have a son, when no man has touched me, and I was never unchaste?"

21 He said, "Thus said your Lord, 'It is easy for Me, and We will make him a sign for humanity, and a mercy from Us. It is a matter already decided.'"

22 So she carried him, and secluded herself with him in a remote place.

23 The labor-pains came upon her, by the trunk of a palm-tree. She said, "I wish I had died before this, and been completely forgotten."

24 Whereupon he called her from beneath her: "Do not worry; your Lord has placed a stream beneath you.

25 And shake the trunk of the palm-tree towards you, and it will drop ripe dates by you."

26 "So eat, and drink, and be consoled. And if you see any human, say, 'I have vowed a fast to the Most Gracious, so I will not speak to any human today.'"

27 Then she came to her people, carrying him. They said, "O Mary, you have done something terrible.

28 O sister of Aaron, your father was not an evil man, and your mother was not a whore."

29 So she pointed to him. They said, "How can we speak to an infant in the crib?"

30 He said, "I am the servant of God. He has given me the Scripture, and made me a prophet.

31 And has made me blessed wherever I may be; and has enjoined on me prayer and charity, so long as I live.

32 And kind to my mother, and He did not make me a disobedient rebel.

33 So Peace is upon me the day I was born, and the day I die, and the Day I get resurrected alive."

34 That is Jesus son of Mary—the Word of truth about which they doubt.

35 It is not for God to have a child—glory be to Him. To have anything done, He says to it, "Be," and it becomes.

36 "God is my Lord and your Lord, so worship Him. That is a straight path."

37 But the various factions differed among themselves. So woe to those who disbelieve from the scene of a tremendous Day.

38 Listen to them and watch for them the Day they come to Us. But the wrong-doers today are completely lost.

39 And warn them of the Day of Regret, when the matter will be concluded. Yet they are heedless, and they do not believe.

40 It is We who will inherit the earth and everyone on it, and to Us they will be returned.

41 And mention in the Scripture Abraham. He was a man of truth, a prophet.

42 He said to his father, "O my father, why do you worship what can neither hear, nor see, nor benefit you in any way?

43 O my father, there has come to me knowledge that never came to you. So follow me, and I will guide you along a straight way.

44 O my father, do not worship the devil. The devil is disobedient to the Most Gracious.

45 O my father, I fear that a punishment from the Most Gracious will afflict you, and you become an ally of the devil."

46 He said, "Are you renouncing my gods, O Abraham? If you do not desist, I will stone you. So leave me alone for a while."

47 He said, "Peace be upon you. I will ask my Lord to forgive you; He has been Kind to me.

48 And I will withdraw from you, and from what you pray to instead of God. And I will pray to my Lord, and I hope I will not be disappointed in my prayer to my Lord."

49 When he withdrew from them, and from what they worship besides God, We granted him Isaac and Jacob. And each We made a prophet.

50 And We gave them freely of Our mercy, and gave them a noble reputation of truth.

51 And mention in the Scripture Moses. He was dedicated. He was a messenger and a prophet.

52 And We called him from the right side of the Mount, and brought him near in communion.

53 And We granted him, out of Our mercy, his brother Aaron, a prophet.

54 And mention in the Scripture Ishmael. He was true to his promise, and was a messenger, a prophet.

55 And he used to enjoin on his people prayer and charity, and he was pleasing to his Lord.

56 And mention in the Scripture Enoch. He was a man of truth, a prophet.

57 And We raised him to a high position.

58 These are some of the prophets God has blessed, from the descendants of Adam, and from those We carried with Noah, and from the descendants of Abraham and Israel, and from those We guided and selected. Whenever the revelations of the Most Gracious are recited to them, they would fall down, prostrating and weeping.

59 But they were succeeded by generations who lost the prayers and followed their appetites. They will meet perdition.

60 Except for those who repent, and believe, and act righteously. These will enter Paradise, and will not be wronged in the least.

61 The Gardens of Eden, promised by the Most Merciful to His servants in the Unseen. His promise will certainly come true.

62 They will hear no nonsense therein, but only peace. And they will have their provision therein, morning and evening.

63 Such is Paradise which We will give as inheritance to those of Our servants who are devout.

64 "We do not descend except by the command of your Lord. His is what is before us, and what is behind us, and what is between them. Your Lord is never forgetful."

65 Lord of the heavens and the earth and what is between them. So worship Him, and persevere in His service. Do you know of anyone equal to Him?

66 And the human being says, "When I am dead, will I be brought back alive?"

67 Does the human being not remember that We created him before, when he was nothing?

68 By your Lord, We will round them up, and the devils, then We will bring them around Hell, on their knees.

69 Then, out of every sect, We will snatch those most defiant to the Most Merciful.

70 We are fully aware of those most deserving to scorch in it.

71 There is not one of you but will go down to it. This has been an unavoidable decree of your Lord.

72 Then We will rescue those who were devout, and leave the wrongdoers in it, on their knees.

73 When Our clear revelations are recited to them, those who disbelieve say to those who believe, "Which of the two parties is better in position, and superior in influence?"

74 How many a generation have We destroyed before them, who surpassed them in riches and splendor?

75 Say, "Whoever is in error, the Most Merciful will lead him on." Until, when they see what they were promised—either the punishment, or the Hour. Then they will know who was in worse position and weaker in forces.

76 God increases in guidance those who accept guidance. And the things that endure—the righteous deeds—have the best reward with your Lord, and the best outcome.

77 Have you seen him who denied Our revelations, and said, "I will be given wealth and children"?

78 Did he look into the future, or did he receive a promise from the Most Merciful?

79 No indeed! We will write what he says, and will keep extending the agony for him.

80 Then We will inherit from him what he speaks of, and he will come to Us alone.

81 And they took, besides God, other gods, to be for them a source of strength.

82 By no means! They will reject their worship of them, and become opponents to them.

83 Have you not considered how We dispatch the devils against the disbelievers, exciting them with incitement?

84 So do not hurry against them. We are counting for them a countdown.

85 On the Day when We will gather the righteous to the Most Merciful, as guests.

86 And herd the sinners into hell, like animals to water.

87 They will have no power of intercession, except for someone who has an agreement with the Most Merciful.

88 And they say, "The Most Merciful has begotten a son."

89 You have come up with something monstrous.

90 At which the heavens almost rupture, and the earth splits, and the mountains fall and crumble.

91 Because they attribute a son to the Most Merciful.

92 It is not fitting for the Most Merciful to have a son.

93 There is none in the heavens and the earth but will come to the Most Merciful as a servant.

94 He has enumerated them, and counted them one by one.

95 And each one of them will come to Him on the Day of Resurrection alone.

96 Those who believe and do righteous deeds, the Most Merciful will give them love.

97 We made it easy in your tongue, in order to deliver good news to the righteous, and to warn with it a hostile people.

98 How many a generation have We destroyed before them? Can you feel a single one of them, or hear from them the slightest whisper?

Ta-Ha (Ta-Ha)

In the name of God, the Gracious, the Merciful.

1 Ta, Ha.

2 We did not reveal the Quran to you to make you suffer.

3 But only as a reminder for him who fears.

4 A revelation from He who created the earth and the high heavens.

5 The Most Merciful; on the Throne He settled.

6 To Him belongs everything in the heavens and the earth, and everything between them, and everything beneath the soil.

7 If you speak aloud—He knows the secret, and the most hidden.

8 God, there is no god but He, His are the Most Beautiful Names.

9 Has the story of Moses reached you?

10 When he saw a fire, he said to his family, "Stay; I have noticed a fire; Perhaps I can bring you a torch therefrom, or find some guidance by the fire."

11 Then, when he reached it, he was called, "O Moses.

12 I—I am your Lord. Take off your shoes. You are in the sacred valley of Tuwa.

13 I have chosen you, so listen to what is revealed.

14 I—I am God. There is no God but I. So serve Me, and practice the prayer for My remembrance.

15 The Hour is coming—but I keep it almost hidden—so that each soul will be paid for what it endeavors.

16 And do not let him who denies it and follows his desire turn you away from it, lest you fall.

17 And what is that in your right-hand, O Moses?"

18 He said, "This is my staff. I lean on it, and herd my sheep with it, and I have other uses for it."

19 He said, "Throw it, O Moses."

20 So he threw it—thereupon it became a moving serpent.

21 He said, "Take hold of it, and do not fear. We will restore it to its original condition.

22 And press your hand to your side; it will come out white, without a blemish—another sign.

23 That We may show you some of Our greatest signs.

24 Go to Pharaoh; He has transgressed."

25 He said, "My Lord, put my heart at peace for me.

26 And ease my task for me.

27 And untie the knot from my tongue.

28 So they can understand my speech.

29 And appoint an assistant for me, from my family.

30 Aaron, my brother.

31 Strengthen me with him.

32 And have him share in my mission.

33 That we may glorify You much.

34 And remember You much.

35 You are always watching over us."

36 He said, "You are granted your request, O Moses.

37 We had favored you another time.

38 When We inspired your mother with the inspiration.

39 'Put him in the chest; then cast him into the river. The river will wash him to shore, where an enemy of Mine and an enemy of his will pick him up. And I have bestowed upon you love from Me, so that you may be reared before My eye.

40 When your sister walked along, and said, 'Shall I tell you about someone who will take care of him?' So We returned you to your mother, that she may be comforted, and not sorrow. And you killed a person, but We saved you from stress; and We tested you thoroughly. And you stayed years among the people of Median. Then you came back, as ordained, O Moses.

41 And I made you for Myself.

42 Go, you and your brother, with My signs, and do not neglect My remembrance.

43 Go to Pharaoh. He has tyrannized.

44 But speak to him nicely. Perhaps he will remember, or have some fear."

45 They said, "Lord, we fear he may persecute us, or become violent."

46 He said, "Do not fear, I am with you, I hear and I see.

47 Approach him and say, 'We are the messengers of your Lord; so let the Children of Israel go with us, and do not torment them. We bring you a sign from your Lord, and peace be upon him who follows guidance.

48 It was revealed to us that the punishment falls upon him who disbelieves and turns away.'"

49 He said, "Who is your Lord, O Moses."

50 He said, "Our Lord is He who gave everything its existence, then guided it."

51 He said, "What about the first generations?"

52 He said, "Knowledge thereof is with my Lord, in a Book. My Lord never errs, nor does He forget."

53 He who made the earth a habitat for you; and traced in it routes for you; and sent down water from the sky, with which We produce pairs of diverse plants.

54 Eat and pasture your livestock. In that are signs for those with understanding.

55 From it We created you, and into it We will return you, and from it We will bring you out another time.

56 We showed him Our signs, all of them, but he denied and refused.

57 He said, "Did you come to us to drive us out of our land with your magic, O Moses?

58 We will produce for you magic like it; so make an appointment between us and you, which we will not miss—neither us, nor you—in a central place."

59 He said, "Your appointment is the day of the festival, so let the people be gathered together at mid-morning."

60 Pharaoh turned away, put together his plan, and then came back.

61 Moses said to them, "Woe to you. Do not fabricate lies against God, or He will destroy you with a punishment. He who invents lies will fail."

62 They disagreed among themselves over their affair, and conferred secretly.

63 They said, "These two are magicians who want to drive you out of your land with their magic, and to abolish your exemplary way of life.

64 So settle your plan, and come as one front. Today, whoever gains the upper hand will succeed."

65 They said, "O Moses, either you throw, or we will be the first to throw."

66 He said, "You throw." And suddenly, their ropes and sticks appeared to him, because of their magic, to be crawling swiftly.

67 So Moses felt apprehensive within himself.

68 We said, "Do not be afraid, you are the uppermost.

69 Now throw down what is in your right hand—it will swallow what they have crafted. What they have crafted is only a magician's trickery. But the magician will not succeed, no matter what he does."

70 And the magicians fell down prostrate. They said, "We have believed in the Lord of Aaron and Moses."

71 He said, "Did you believe in him before I have given you permission? He must be your chief, who has taught you magic. I will cut off your hands and your feet on alternate sides, and I will crucify you on the trunks of the palm-trees. Then you will know which of us is more severe in punishment, and more lasting."

72 They said, "We will not prefer you to the proofs that have come to us, and Him who created us. So issue whatever judgment you wish to issue. You can only rule in this lowly life.

73 We have believed in our Lord, so that He may forgive us our sins, and the magic you have compelled us to practice. God is Better, and more Lasting."

74 Whoever comes to his Lord guilty, for him is Hell, where he neither dies nor lives.

75 But whoever comes to Him a believer, having worked righteousness—these will have the highest ranks.

76 The Gardens of Perpetuity, beneath which rivers flow, dwelling therein forever. That is the reward for him who purifies himself.

77 And We inspired Moses: "Travel by night with My servants, and strike for them a dry path across the sea, not fearing being overtaken, nor worrying."

78 Pharaoh pursued them with his troops, but the sea overwhelmed them, and completely engulfed them.

79 Pharaoh misled his people, and did not guide them.

80 O Children of Israel! We have delivered you from your enemy, and promised you by the right side of the Mount, and sent down to you manna and quails.

81 Eat of the good things We have provided for you, but do not be excessive therein, lest My wrath descends upon you. He upon whom My wrath descends has fallen.

82 And I am Forgiving towards him who repents, believes, acts righteously, and then remains guided.

83 "And what made you rush ahead of your people, O Moses?"

84 He said, "They are following in my footsteps; and I hurried on to You, my Lord, that you may be pleased."

85 He said, "We have tested your people in your absence, and the Samarian misled them."

86 So Moses returned to his people, angry and disappointed. He said, "O my people, did your Lord not promise you a good promise? Was the time too long for you? Or did you want wrath from your Lord to descend upon you, so you broke your promise to me?"

87 They said, "We did not break our promise to you by our choice, but we were made to carry loads of the people's ornaments, and we cast them in. That was what the Samarian suggested."

88 So he produced for them a calf—a mere body which lowed. And they said, "This is your god, and the god of Moses, but he has forgotten."

89 Did they not see that it cannot return a word to them, and has no power to harm them or benefit them?

90 Aaron had said to them before, "O my people, you are being tested by this. And your Lord is the Merciful, so follow me, and obey my command."

91 They said, "We will not give up our devotion to it, until Moses returns to us."

92 He said, "O Aaron, what prevented you, when you saw them going astray.

93 From following me? Did you disobey my command?"

94 He said, "Son of my mother, do not seize me by my beard or my head. I feared you would say, 'You have caused division among the Children of Israel, and did not regard my word.'"

95 He said, "What do you have to say, O Samarian?"

96 He said, "I saw what they did not see, so I grasped a handful from the Messenger's traces, and I flung it away. Thus my soul prompted me."

97 He said, "Begone! Your lot in this life is to say, 'No contact.' And you have an appointment that you will not miss. Now look at your god that you remained devoted to—we will burn it up, and then blow it away into the sea, as powder."

98 Surely your god is God, the One besides whom there is no other god. He comprehends everything in knowledge.

99 Thus We narrate to you reports of times gone by; and We have given you a message from Our Presence.

100 Whoever turns away from it will carry on the Day of Resurrection a burden.

101 Abiding therein forever. And wretched is their burden on the Day of Resurrection.

102 On the Day when the Trumpet is blown—We will gather the sinners on that Day, blue.

103 Murmuring among themselves: "You have lingered only for ten."

104 We are fully aware of what they say, when the most exemplary of them in conduct will say, "You have lingered only a day."

105 And they ask you about the mountains. Say, "My Lord will crumble them utterly."

106 And leave them desolate waste.

107 You will see in them neither crookedness, nor deviation."

108 On that Day, they will follow the caller, without any deviation. Voices will be hushed before the Merciful, and you will hear nothing but murmur.

109 On that Day, intercession will not avail, except for him permitted by the Merciful, and whose words He has approved.

110 He knows what is before them and what is behind them, and they cannot comprehend Him in their knowledge.

111 Faces will be humbled before the Living, the Eternal. Whoever carries injustice will despair.

112 But whoever has done righteous deeds, while being a believer—will fear neither injustice, nor grievance.

113 Thus We have revealed it an Arabic Quran, and We have diversified the warnings in it, that perhaps they would become righteous, or it may produce a lesson for them.

114 Exalted is God, the True King. Do not be hasty with the Quran before its inspiration to you is concluded, and say, "My Lord, increase me in knowledge."

115 And We covenanted with Adam before, but he forgot, and We found in him no resolve.

116 And when We said to the angels, "Bow down to Adam." They bowed down, except for Satan; he refused.

117 We said, "O Adam, this is an enemy to you and to your wife. So do not let him make you leave the Garden, for then you will suffer.

118 In it you will never go hungry, nor be naked.

119 Nor will you be thirsty in it, nor will you swelter."

120 But Satan whispered to him. He said, "O Adam, shall I show you the Tree of Immortality, and a kingdom that never decays?"

121 And so they ate from it; whereupon their bodies became visible to them, and they started covering themselves with the leaves of the Garden. Thus Adam disobeyed his Lord, and fell.

122 But then his Lord recalled him, and pardoned him, and guided him.

123 He said, "Go down from it, altogether; some of you enemies of some others. But whenever guidance comes to you from Me, whoever follows My guidance, will not go astray, nor suffer.

124 But whoever turns away from My Reminder, for him is a confined life. And We will raise him on the Day of Resurrection blind."

125 He will say, "My Lord, why did You raise me blind, though I was seeing?"

126 He will say, "Just as Our revelations came to you, and you forgot them, today you will be forgotten."

127 Thus We recompense him who transgresses and does not believe in the revelations of his Lord. The punishment of the Hereafter is more severe, and more lasting.

128 Is it not instructive to them, how many generations before them We destroyed, in whose settlements they walk? Surely in that are signs for people of understanding.

129 Were it not for a word that issued from your Lord, the inevitable would have happened, but there is an appointed term.

130 So bear patiently what they say, and celebrate the praises of your Lord before the rising of the sun, and before its setting. And during the hours of the night glorify Him, and at the borders of the day, that you may be satisfied.

131 And do not extend your glance towards what We have given some classes of them to enjoy—the splendor of the life of this world—that We may test them thereby. Your Lord's provision is better, and more lasting.

132 And exhort your people to pray, and patiently adhere to it. We ask of you no sustenance, but it is We who sustain you. The good ending is that for righteousness.

133 And they say, "Why does he not bring us a miracle from his Lord?" Were they not given enough miracles in the former scriptures?

134 Had We destroyed them with a punishment before him, they would have said, "Our Lord, if only You had sent us a messenger, we would have followed Your revelations before we were humiliated and disgraced."

135 Say, "Everybody is waiting, so wait. You will know who the people of the straight path are, and who is rightly-guided.

The Pilgrimage (al-Hajj)

In the name of God, the Gracious, the Merciful.

1 O people, be conscious of your Lord. The quaking of the Hour is a tremendous thing.

2 On the Day when you will see it: every nursing mother will discard her infant, and every pregnant woman will abort her load, and you will see the people drunk, even though they are not drunk—but the punishment of God is severe.

3 Among the people is he who argues about God without knowledge, and follows every defiant devil.

4 It was decreed for him, that whoever follows him—he will misguide him, and lead him to the torment of the Blaze.

5 O people! If you are in doubt about the Resurrection—We created you from dust, then from a small drop, then from a clinging clot, then from a lump of flesh, partly developed and partly undeveloped. In order to clarify things for you. And We settle in the wombs whatever We will for a designated term, and then We bring you out as infants, until you reach your full strength. And some of you will pass away, and some of you will be returned to the vilest age, so that he may not know, after having known. And you see the earth still; but when We send down water on it, it vibrates, and swells, and grows all kinds of lovely pairs.

6 That is because God is the truth, and because He gives life to the dead, and because He is Capable of everything.

7 And because the Hour is coming—there is no doubt about it—and because God will resurrect those in the graves.

8 And among the people is he who argues about God without knowledge, or guidance, or an enlightening scripture.

9 Turning aside in contempt, to lead away from the path of God. He will have humiliation in this world, and on the Day of Resurrection We will make him taste the agony of burning.

10 That is for what your hands have advanced, and because God is not unjust to the servants.

11 And among the people is he who worships God on edge. When something good comes his way, he is content with it. But when an ordeal strikes him, he makes a turnaround. He loses this world and the next. That is the obvious loss.

12 He invokes, instead of God, what can neither harm him nor benefit him. That is the far straying.

13 He invokes one whose harm is closer than his benefit. What a miserable master. What a miserable companion.

14 God will admit those who believe and do righteous deeds into Gardens beneath which rivers flow. God does whatever He wills.

15 Whoever thinks that God will not help him in this life and in the Hereafter—let him turn to heaven, then sever, and see if his cunning eliminates what enrages him.

16 Thus We revealed it as clarifying signs, and God guides whomever He wills.

17 Those who believe, and those who are Jewish, and the Sabeans, and the Christians, and the Zoroastrians, and the Polytheists—God will judge between them on the Day of Resurrection. God is witness to all things.

18 Do you not realize that to God prostrates everyone in the heavens and everyone on earth, and the sun, and the moon, and the stars, and the mountains, and the trees, and the animals, and many of the people? But many are justly deserving of punishment. Whomever God shames, there is none to honor him. God does whatever He wills.

19 Here are two adversaries feuding regarding their Lord. As for those who disbelieve, garments of fire will be tailored for them, and scalding water will be poured over their heads.

20 Melting their insides and their skins.

21 And they will have maces of iron.

22 Whenever they try to escape the gloom, they will be driven back to it: "Taste the suffering of burning."

23 But God will admit those who believe and do good deeds into Gardens beneath which rivers flow. They will be decorated therein with bracelets of gold and pearls, and their garments therein will be of silk.

24 They were guided to purity of speech. They were guided to the path of the Most Praised.

25 As for those who disbelieve and repel from God's path and from the Sacred Mosque—which We have designated for all mankind equally, whether residing therein or passing through—and seek to commit sacrilege therein—We will make him taste of a painful punishment.

26 We showed Abraham the location of the House: "Do not associate anything with Me; and purify My House for those who circle around, and those who stand to pray, and those who kneel and prostrate."

27 And announce the pilgrimage to humanity. They will come to you on foot, and on every transport. They will come from every distant point.

28 That they may witness the benefits for themselves, and celebrate the name of God during the appointed days, for providing them with the animal livestock. So eat from it, and feed the unfortunate poor.

29 Then let them perform their acts of cleansing, and fulfill their vows, and circle around the Ancient House.

30 All that. Whoever venerates the sanctities of God—it is good for him with his Lord. All livestock are permitted to you, except what is recited to you. So stay away from the abomination of idols, and stay away from perjury.

31 Being true to God, without associating anything with Him. Whoever associates anything with God—it is as though he has fallen from the sky, and is snatched by the birds, or is swept away by the wind to a distant abyss.

32 So it is. Whoever venerates the sacraments of God—it is from the piety of the hearts.

33 In them are benefits for you until a certain time. Then their place is by the Ancient House.

34 We have appointed a rite for every nation, that they may commemorate God's name over the livestock He has provided for them. Your God is One God, so to Him submit, and announce good news to the humble.

35 Those whose hearts tremble when God is mentioned, and those who endure what has befallen them, and those who perform the prayer and spend from what We have provided for them.

36 We have made the animal offerings emblems of God for you. In them is goodness for you. So pronounce God's name upon them as they line up. Then, when they have fallen on their sides, eat of them and feed the contented and the beggar. Thus We have subjected them to you, that you may be thankful.

37 Neither their flesh, nor their blood, ever reaches God. What reaches Him is the righteousness from you. Thus He subdued them to you, that you may glorify God for guiding you. And give good news to the charitable.

38 God defends those who believe. God does not love any ungrateful traitor.

39 Permission is given to those who are fought against, and God is Able to give them victory.

40 Those who were unjustly evicted from their homes, merely for saying, "Our Lord is God." Were it not that God repels people by means of others: monasteries, churches, synagogues, and mosques—where the name of God is mentioned much—would have been demolished. God supports whoever supports Him. God is Strong and Mighty.

41 Those who, when We empower them in the land, observe the prayer, and give regular charity, and command what is right, and forbid what is wrong. To God belongs the outcome of events.

42 If they deny you—before them the people of Noah, and Aad, and Thamood also denied.

43 And the people of Abraham, and the people of Lot.

44 And the inhabitants of Median. And Moses was denied. Then I reprieved those who disbelieved, but then I seized them. So how was My rejection?

45 How many a town have We destroyed while it was doing wrong? They lie in ruins; with stilled wells, and lofty mansions.

46 Have they not journeyed in the land, and had minds to reason with, or ears to listen with? It is not the eyes that go blind, but it is the hearts, within the chests, that go blind.

47 And they ask you to hasten the punishment. But God never breaks His promise. A day with your Lord is like a thousand years of your count.

48 How many a town have I reprieved, although it was unjust? Then I seized it. To Me is the destination.

49 Say, "O people, I am only a plain warner to you."

50 Those who believe and work righteousness—for them is forgiveness and a generous provision.

51 But those who strive against Our revelations—these are the inmates of Hell.

52 We never sent a messenger before you, or a prophet, but when he had a desire Satan interfered in his wishes. But God nullifies what Satan interjects, and God affirms His revelations. God is Omniscient and Wise.

53 In order to make Satan's suggestions a trial for those whose hearts are diseased, and those whose hearts are hardened. The wrongdoers are in profound discord.

54 And so that those endowed with knowledge may know that it is the truth from your Lord, and so believe in it, and their hearts soften to it. God guides those who believe to a straight path.

55 Those who disbelieve will continue to be hesitant about it, until the Hour comes upon them suddenly, or there comes to them the torment of a desolate Day.

56 Sovereignty on that Day belongs to God; He will judge between them. Those who believe and do good deeds will be in the Gardens of Bliss.

57 But those who disbelieve and reject Our revelations—these will have a humiliating punishment.

58 Those who emigrate in God's cause, then get killed, or die, God will provide them with fine provisions. God is the Best of Providers.

59 He will admit them an admittance that will please them. God is Knowing and Clement.

60 That is so! Whoever retaliates similarly to the affliction he was made to suffer, and then he is wronged again, God will definitely assist him. God is Pardoning and Forgiving.

61 That is because God merges the night into the day, and He merges the day into the night, and because God is Hearing and Seeing.

62 That is because God is the Reality, and what they invoke besides Him is vanity, and because God is the Sublime, the Grand.

63 Do you not see that God sends down water from the sky, and the land becomes green? God is Kind and Aware.

64 To Him belongs everything in the heavens and everything on earth. God is the Rich, the Praised.

65 Do you not see that God made everything on earth subservient to you? How the ships sail at sea by His command? That He holds up the sky lest it falls on earth—except by His permission? God is Gracious towards the people, Most Merciful.

66 And it is He who gives you life, then makes you die, then revives you. The human being is unappreciative.

67 For every congregation We have appointed acts of devotion, which they observe. So do not let them dispute with you in this matter. And invite to your Lord; you are upon a straight guidance.

68 But if they dispute with you, say, "God is fully aware of what you do."

69 God will judge between you on the Day of Resurrection regarding what you disagree about.

70 Do you not know that God knows everything in the heavens and the earth? This is in a book. That is easy for God.

71 Yet they worship, besides God, things for which He sent down no warrant, and what they have no knowledge of. There is no savior for the transgressors.

72 And when Our Clear Verses are recited to them, you will recognize disgust on the faces of those who disbelieve. They nearly assault those who recite to them Our Verses. Say, "Shall I inform you of something worse than that? The Fire! God has promised it to those who disbelieve. And what a wretched outcome!"

73 O people! A parable is presented, so listen to it: Those you invoke besides God will never create a fly, even if they banded together for that purpose. And if the fly steals anything from them, they cannot recover it from it. Weak are the pursuer and the pursued.

74 They do not value God as He should be valued. God is Strong and Powerful.

75 God chooses messengers from among the angels, and from among the people. God is Hearing and Seeing.

76 He knows what is before them, and what is behind them. To God all matters are referred.

77 O you who believe! Kneel, and prostrate, and worship your Lord, and do good deeds, so that you may succeed.

78 And strive for God, with the striving due to Him. He has chosen you, and has not burdened you in religion—the faith of your father Abraham. It is he who named you Muslims before, and in this. So that the Messenger may be a witness over you, and you may be witnesses over the people. So pray regularly, and give regular charity, and cleave to God. He is your Protector. What an excellent Protector, and what an excellent Helper.

The Poets (ash-Shu'ara')

In the name of God, the Gracious, the Merciful.

1 Ta, Seen, Meem.

2 These are the Verses of the Clarifying Book.

3 Perhaps you will destroy yourself with grief, because they do not become believers.

4 If We will, We can send down upon them a sign from heaven, at which their necks will stay bent in humility.

5 No fresh reminder comes to them from the Most Merciful, but they turn their backs at it.

6 They have denied the truth, but soon will come to them the news of what they ridiculed.

7 Have they not seen the earth, and how many beautiful pairs We produced therein?

8 Surely in this is a sign, but most of them are not believers.

9 Most surely, your Lord is the Almighty, the Merciful.

10 Your Lord called to Moses, "Go to the tyrannical people.

11 The people of Pharaoh. Will they not fear?"

12 He said, "My Lord, I fear they will reject me.

13 And I become stressed, and my tongue is not fluent, so send Aaron too.

14 And they have a charge against me, so I fear they will kill me."

15 He said, "No. Go, both of you, with Our proofs. We will be with you, listening.

16 Go to Pharaoh, and say, 'We are the Messengers of the Lord of the Worlds.

17 Let the Children of Israel go with us.'"

18 He said, "Did we not raise you among us as a child, and you stayed among us for many of your years?

19 And you committed that deed you committed, and you were ungrateful."

20 He said, "I did it then, when I was of those astray.

21 And I fled from you when I feared you; but my Lord gave me wisdom, and made me one of the messengers.

22 Is that the favor you taunt me with, although you have enslaved the Children of Israel?"

23 Pharaoh said, "And what is the Lord of the Worlds?"

24 He said, "The Lord of the heavens and the earth, and everything between them, if you are aware."

25 He said to those around him, "Do you not hear?"

26 He said, "Your Lord and the Lord of your ancestors of old."

27 He said, "This messenger of yours, who is sent to you, is crazy."

28 He said, "Lord of the East and the West, and everything between them, if you understand."

29 He said, "If you accept any god other than me, I will make you a prisoner."

30 He said, "What if I bring you something convincing?"

31 He said, "Bring it, if you are being truthful."

32 So he cast his staff; and it was a serpent, plain to see.

33 And he pulled his hand; and it was white, for all to see.

34 He said to the dignitaries around him, "This is a skilled magician.

35 He intends to drive you out of your land with his magic, so what do you recommend?"

36 They said, "Delay him and his brother, and send recruiters to the cities.

37 To bring you every experienced magician."

38 So the magicians were gathered for the appointment on a specified day.

39 And it was said to the people, "Are you all gathered?

40 That we may follow the magicians, if they are the winners."

41 When the magicians arrived, they said to Pharaoh, "Is there a reward for us, if we are the winners?"

42 He said, "Yes, and you will be among those favored."

43 Moses said to them, "Present what you intend to present."

44 So they threw their ropes and their sticks, and said, "By the majesty of Pharaoh, we will be the winners."

45 Then Moses threw his staff, and behold, it began swallowing their trickery.

46 And the magicians fell down prostrating.

47 They said, "We have believed in the Lord of the Worlds."

48 The Lord of Moses and Aaron."

49 He said, "Did you believe in Him before I have given you permission? He must be your chief, who taught you magic. You will soon know. I will cut off your hands and feet on opposite sides, and I will crucify you all."

50 They said, "No problem. To our Lord we will return.

51 We are eager for our Lord to forgive us our sins, since we are the first of the believers."

52 And We inspired Moses: "Travel with My servants by night. You will be followed."

53 Pharaoh sent heralds to the cities.

54 "These are a small gang.

55 And they are enraging us.

56 But we are a vigilant multitude."

57 So We drove them out of gardens and springs.

58 And treasures and noble dwellings.

59 So it was. And We made the Children of Israel inherit them.

60 And they pursued them at sunrise.

61 When the two groups sighted each other, the followers of Moses said, "We are being overtaken."

62 He said, "No; my Lord is with me, He will guide me."

63 We inspired Moses: "Strike the sea with your staff." Whereupon it parted, and each part was like a huge hill.

64 And there We brought the others near.

65 And We saved Moses and those with him, all together.

66 Then We drowned the others.

67 In that there is a sign, but most of them are not believers.

68 Surely, your Lord is the Almighty, the Merciful.

69 And relate to them the story of Abraham.

70 When he said to his father and his people, "What do you worship?"
71 They said, "We worship idols, and we remain devoted to them."
72 He said, "Do they hear you when you pray?
73 Or do they benefit you, or harm you?"
74 They said, "But we found our ancestors doing so."
75 He said, "Have you considered what you worship.
76 You and your ancient ancestors?
77 They are enemies to me, but not so the Lord of the Worlds.
78 He who created me, and guides me.
79 He who feeds me, and waters me.
80 And when I get sick, He heals me.
81 He who makes me die, and then revives me.
82 He who, I hope, will forgive my sins on the Day of the Reckoning."
83 "My Lord! Grant me wisdom, and include me with the righteous.
84 And give me a reputation of truth among the others.
85 And make me of the inheritors of the Garden of Bliss.
86 And forgive my father—he was one of the misguided.
87 And do not disgrace me on the Day they are resurrected.
88 The Day when neither wealth nor children will help.
89 Except for him who comes to God with a sound heart."
90 And Paradise will be brought near for the righteous.
91 And the Blaze will be displayed to the deviators.
92 And it will be said to them, "Where are those you used to worship?"
93 Besides God? Can they help you, or help themselves?"
94 Then they will be toppled into it, together with the seducers.
95 And the soldiers of Satan, all of them.
96 They will say, as they feud in it.
97 "By God, We were in evident error.
98 For equating you with the Lord of the Worlds.
99 No one misled us except the sinners.

100 Now we have no intercessors.

101 And no sincere friend.

102 If only we could have another chance, we would be among the faithful."

103 Surely in this is a sign, but most of them are not believers.

104 Your Lord is the Almighty, the Merciful.

105 The people of Noah disbelieved the messengers.

106 Their brother Noah said to them, "Do you not fear?

107 I am to you a faithful messenger.

108 So fear God, and obey me.

109 I ask of you no payment for this. My payment is only from the Lord of the Worlds.

110 So fear God, and obey me."

111 They said, "Shall we believe in you, when it is the lowliest who follow you?"

112 He said, "What do I know about what they do?

113 Their account rests only with my Lord, if you have sense.

114 And I am not about to drive away the believers.

115 I am only a clear warner."

116 They said, "If you do not refrain, O Noah, you will be stoned."

117 He said, "My Lord, my people have denied me.

118 So judge between me and them decisively, and deliver me and the believers who are with me.

119 So We delivered him and those with him in the laden Ark.

120 Then We drowned the rest.

121 In that is a sign, but most of them are not believers.

122 Your Lord is the Almighty, the Merciful.

123 Aad disbelieved the messengers.

124 When their brother Hud said to them, "Do you not fear?

125 I am to you a faithful messenger.

126 So fear God, and obey me.

127 I ask of you no payment for this. My payment is only from the Lord of the Worlds.

128 Do you build a monument on every height for vanity's sake?

129 And you set up fortresses, hoping to live forever?

130 And when you strike, you strike mercilessly?

131 So fear God, and obey me.

132 And reverence Him, who supplied you with everything you know.

133 He supplied you with livestock and children.

134 And gardens and springs.

135 I fear for you the punishment of an awesome Day."

136 They said, "It is the same for us, whether you lecture us, or do not lecture.

137 This is nothing but morals of the ancients.

138 And we will not be punished."

139 So they denied him, and We destroyed them. Surely in this is a sign, but most of them are not believers.

140 Your Lord is the Almighty, the Merciful.

141 Thamood disbelieved the messengers.

142 When their brother Saleh said to them, "Do you not fear?

143 I am to you a faithful messenger.

144 So fear God, and obey me.

145 I ask of you no payment for it. My payment is only from the Lord of the Worlds.

146 Will you be left secure in what is here?

147 In gardens and springs?

148 And fields, and palm-trees whose fruits are delicious?

149 And you skillfully carve houses in the mountains?

150 So fear God, and obey me.

151 And do not obey the command of the extravagant.

152 Who spread turmoil on earth, and do not reform."

153 They said, "You are surely one of the bewitched.

154 You are nothing but a man like us. So bring us a sign, if you are truthful.

155 He said, "This is a she-camel; she has her turn of drinking, and you have your turn of drinking—on a specified day.

156 And do not touch her with harm, lest the punishment of a great day seizes you."

157 But they slaughtered her, and became full of remorse.

158 So the punishment overtook them. Surely in this is a sign, but most of them are not believers.

159 Your Lord is the Almighty, the Merciful.

160 The people of Lot disbelieved the messengers.

161 When their brother Lot said to them, "Do you not fear?

162 I am to you a faithful messenger.

163 So fear God, and obey me.

164 I ask of you no payment for it. My payment is only from the Lord of the Worlds.

165 Do you approach the males of the world?

166 And forsake the wives your Lord created for you? Indeed, you are intrusive people."

167 They said, "Unless you refrain, O Lot, you will be expelled."

168 He said, "I certainly deplore your conduct."

169 "My Lord, save me and my family from what they do."

170 So We saved him and his family, altogether.

171 Except for an old woman among those who tarried.

172 Then We destroyed the others.

173 And We rained down on them a rain. Dreadful is the rain of those forewarned.

174 Surely in this is a sign, but most of them are not believers.

175 Your Lord is the Almighty, the Merciful.

176 The People of the Woods disbelieved the messengers.

177 When Shuaib said to them, "Do you not fear?

178 I am to you a trustworthy messenger.

179 So fear God, and obey me.

180 I ask of you no payment for it. My payment is only from the Lord of the Worlds.

181 Give full measure, and do not cheat.

182 And weigh with accurate scales.

183 And do not defraud people of their belongings, and do not work corruption in the land.

184 And fear Him who created you and the masses of old."

185 They said, "You are one of those bewitched.

186 And you are nothing but a man like us; and we think that you are a liar.

187 So bring down on us pieces from the sky, if you are truthful."

188 He said, "My Lord is Well Aware of what you do."

189 But they denied him. So the punishment of the day of gloom gripped them. It was the punishment of a great day.

190 Surely in this is a sign, but most of them are not believers.

191 Your Lord is the Almighty, the Merciful.

192 It is a revelation from the Lord of the Worlds.

193 The Honest Spirit came down with it.

194 Upon your heart, that you may be one of the warners.

195 In a clear Arabic tongue.

196 And it is in the scriptures of the ancients.

197 Is it not a sign for them that the scholars of the Children of Israel recognized it?

198 Had We revealed it to one of the foreigners.

199 And he had recited it to them, they still would not have believed in it.

200 Thus We make it pass through the hearts of the guilty.

201 They will not believe in it until they witness the painful punishment.

202 It will come to them suddenly, while they are unaware.

203 Then they will say, "Are we given any respite?"

204 Do they seek to hasten Our punishment?

205 Have you considered: if We let them enjoy themselves for some years.

206 Then there comes to them what they were promised.

207 Of what avail to them will be their past enjoyments?

208 Never did We destroy a town, but it had warners.

209 As a reminder—We are never unjust.

210 It was not the devils that revealed it.

211 It is not in their interests, nor in their power.

212 They are barred from hearing.

213 So do not pray to another god with God, else you will be of those tormented.

214 And warn your close relatives.

215 And lower your wing to those of the believers who follow you.

216 And if they disobey you, say, "I am innocent of what you do."

217 And put your trust in the Almighty, the Merciful.

218 He Who sees you when you rise.

219 And your devotions amidst the worshipers.

220 He is indeed the Hearer, the Aware.

221 Shall I inform you upon whom the devils descend?

222 They descend upon every sinful liar.

223 They give ear, and most of them are liars.

224 And as for the poets—the deviators follow them.

225 Do you not see how they ramble in every style?

226 And how they say what they do not do?

227 Except for those who believe, and do good deeds, and remember God frequently, and defend themselves after they are wronged. As for those who do wrong, they will know by what overturning they will be overturned.

History (al-Qasas)

In the name of God, the Gracious, the Merciful.

1 Ta, Seen, Meem.

2 These are the Verses of the Clear Book.

3 We narrate to you from the history of Moses and Pharaoh—in truth—for people who believe.

4 Pharaoh exalted himself in the land, and divided its people into factions. He persecuted a group of them, slaughtering their sons, while sparing their daughters. He was truly a corrupter.

5 But We desired to favor those who were oppressed in the land, and to make them leaders, and to make them the inheritors.

6 And to establish them in the land; and to show Pharaoh, Hamaan, and their troops, the very thing they feared.

7 We inspired the mother of Moses: "Nurse him; then, when you fear for him, cast him into the river, and do not fear, nor grieve; We will return him to you, and make him one of the messengers."

8 Pharaoh's household picked him up, to be an opponent and a sorrow for them. Pharaoh, Hamaan, and their troops were sinners.

9 Pharaoh's wife said, "An eye's delight for me and for you. Do not kill him; perhaps he will be useful to us, or we may adopt him as a son." But they did not foresee.

10 The heart of Moses' mother became vacant. She was about to disclose him, had We not steadied her heart, that she may remain a believer.

11 She said to his sister, "Trail him." So she watched him from afar, and they were unaware.

12 We forbade him breastfeeding at first. So she said, "Shall I tell you about a family that can raise him for you, and will look after him?"

13 Thus We returned him to his mother, that she may be comforted, and not grieve, and know that God's promise is true. But most of them do not know.

14 And when he reached his maturity, and became established, We gave him wisdom and knowledge. Thus do We reward the virtuous.

15 Once he entered the city, unnoticed by its people. He found in it two men fighting—one of his own sect, and one from his enemies. The one of his sect solicited his assistance against the one from his enemies; so Moses punched him, and put an end to him. He said, "This is of Satan's doing; he is an enemy that openly misleads."

16 He said, "My Lord, I have wronged myself, so forgive me." So He forgave him. He is the Forgiver, the Merciful.

17 He said, "My Lord, in as much as you have favored me, I will never be a supporter of the criminals."

18 The next morning, he went about in the city, fearful and vigilant, when the man who had sought his assistance the day before was shouting out to him. Moses said to him, "You are clearly a troublemaker."

19 As he was about to strike the one who was their enemy, he said, "O Moses, do you intend to kill me, as you killed someone yesterday? You only want to be a bully in the land, and do not want to be a peacemaker."

20 And a man came from the farthest part of the city running. He said, "O Moses, the authorities are considering killing you, so leave; I am giving you good advice."

21 So he left, fearful and vigilant. He said, "My Lord, deliver me from the wrongdoing people."

22 As he headed towards Median, he said, "Perhaps my Lord will guide me to the right way."

23 And when he arrived at the waters of Median, he found there a crowd of people drawing water, and he noticed two women waiting on the side. He said, "What is the matter with you?" They said, "We cannot draw water until the shepherds depart, and our father is a very old man."

24 So he drew water for them, and then withdrew to the shade, and said, "My Lord, I am in dire need of whatever good you might send down to me."

25 Then, one of the two women approached him, walking bashfully. She said, "My father is calling you, to reward you for drawing water for us." And when he came to him, and told him the story, he said, "Do not fear, you have escaped from the wrongdoing people."

26 One of the two women said, "Father, hire him; the best employee for you is the strong and trustworthy."

27 He said, "I want to marry you to one of these two daughters of mine, provided you work for me for eight years. But if you complete ten, that is up to you. I do not intend to impose any hardship on you. You will find me, God willing, one of the righteous."

28 He said, "Let this be an agreement between you and me. Whichever of the two terms I fulfill, there shall be no reprisal against me; and God is witness over what we say."

29 When Moses had completed the term, and departed with his family, he noticed a fire by the side of the Mount. He said to his family, "Stay here, I have glimpsed a fire. Perhaps I can bring you some information from there, or an ember from the fire, that you may warm yourselves."

30 When he reached it, he was called from the right side of the valley, at the Blessed Spot, from the bush: "O Moses, it is I, God, the Lord of the Worlds.

31 Throw down your staff." And when he saw it wiggling, as if it were possessed, he turned his back to flee, and did not look back. "O Moses, come forward, and do not fear, you are perfectly safe.

32 Put your hand inside your pocket, and it will come out white, without blemish. And press your arm to your side, against fear. These are two proofs from your Lord, to Pharaoh and his dignitaries. They are truly sinful people."

33 He said, "My Lord, I have killed one of them, and I fear they will kill me.

34 And my brother Aaron, he is more eloquent than me, so send him with me, to help me, and to confirm my words, for I fear they will reject me."

35 He said, "We will strengthen your arm with your brother, and We will give you authority, so they will not touch you. By virtue of Our signs, you and those who follow you will be the triumphant."

36 But when Moses came to them with Our signs, clear and manifest, they said, "This is nothing but fabricated magic, and We never heard of this from our ancestors of old."

37 Moses said, "My Lord is well aware of him who brings guidance from Him, and him who will have the sequel of the abode. The wrongdoers will not succeed."

38 Pharaoh said, "O nobles, I know of no god for you other than me. So fire-up the bricks for me O Hamaan, and build me a tower, that I may ascend to the God of Moses, though I think he is a liar."

39 He and his troops acted arrogantly in the land, with no justification. They thought they would not be returned to Us.

40 So We seized him, and his troops, and We threw them into the sea. Observe, therefore, what was the end of the oppressors.

41 And We made them leaders calling to the Fire. And on Resurrection Day, they will not be saved.

42 And We pursued them in this world with a curse. And on Resurrection Day, they will be among the despised.

43 We gave Moses the Scripture after We had annihilated the previous generations; as an illumination for mankind, and guidance, and mercy, so that they may remember.

44 You were not on the Western Side when We decreed the command to Moses, nor were you among the witnesses.

45 But We established many generations, and time took its toll on them. Nor were you among the people of Median, reciting Our revelations to them. But We kept sending messengers.

46 Nor were you by the side of the Mount when We proclaimed. Rather, it was a mercy from your Lord, that you may warn people who received no warner before you, so that they may take heed.

47 Otherwise, if a calamity befell them as a result of what their hands have perpetrated, they would say, "Our Lord, if only You had sent us a messenger, we would have followed Your revelations, and been among the believers."

48 But when the truth came to them from Us, they said, "If only he was given the like of what was given to Moses." Did they not disbelieve in what was given to Moses in the past? They said, "Two works of magic backing one another." And they said, "We are disbelieving in both."

49 Say, "Then bring a scripture from God, more conductive to guidance than both, and I will follow it, if you are truthful."

50 But if they fail to respond to you, know that they follow their fancies. And who is more lost than him who follows his fancy without guidance from God? God does not guide the unjust people.

51 We have delivered the Word to them, that they may remember.

52 Those to whom We gave the Scripture before it believe in it.

53 When it is recited to them, they say, "We have believed in it; it is the truth from our Lord; we were Muslims prior to it."

54 These will be given their reward twice, because they persevered; and they counter evil with good; and from Our provisions to them, they give.

55 And when they hear vain talk, they avoid it, and say, "We have our deeds, and you have your deeds; peace be upon you; we do not desire the ignorant."

56 You cannot guide whom you love, but God guides whom He wills, and He knows best those who are guided.

57 And they say, "If we follow the guidance with you, we will be snatched from our land." Did We not establish for them a Safe Sanctuary, to which are brought all kinds of fruits, as provision from Ourselves? But most of them do not know.

58 And how many a city did We destroy for turning unappreciative of its livelihood? Here are their homes, uninhabited after them, except for a few. And We became the Inheritors.

59 Your Lord never destroys cities without first sending a messenger in their midst, reciting to them Our revelations. And We never destroy the cities, unless their people are wrongdoers.

60 Whatever thing you are given is but the material of this world, and its glitter. But what is with God is better, and longer lasting. Do you not comprehend?

61 Can someone to whom We have made a fine promise—which he will attain—be equal to someone to whom We have given enjoyments in this world, but who will be, on Resurrection Day, among the arraigned?

62 On the Day when He will call to them, and say, "Where are My associates whom you used to claim?"

63 Those against whom the sentence is justified will say, "Our Lord, these are they whom we misled. We misled them, as we were misled. We beg Your forgiveness; it was not us they used to worship."

64 And it will be said, "Call on your partners." And they will call on them, but they will not respond to them. And they will see the suffering. If only they were guided.

65 On the Day when He will call to them, and say, "What did you answer the Messengers?"

66 They will be blinded by the facts on that Day, and they will not question each other.

67 But he who repents, and believes, and does righteous deeds, may well be among the winners.

68 Your Lord creates whatever He wills, and He chooses. The choice is not theirs. Glory be to God, and exalted be He above the associations they make.

69 And your Lord knows what their hearts conceal, and what they reveal.

70 And He is God. There is no god but He. To Him belongs all praise in this life, and in the next. And His is the decision, and to Him you will be returned.

71 Say, "Have you considered? Had God made the night perpetual over you until the Day of Resurrection, which god other than God will bring you illumination? Do you not hear?"

72 Say, "Have you considered? Had God made the day perpetual over you until the Day of Resurrection, which god other than God will bring you night to rest in? Do you not see?"

73 It is out of His mercy that He made for you the night and the day, that you may rest in it, and seek some of His bounty; and that you may give thanks.

74 On the Day when He will call to them, and say, "Where are My associates whom you used to claim?"

75 And We will draw out from every community a witness, and say, "Produce your evidence." Then they will realize that the truth is God's, and those they used to invent have forsaken them.

76 Quaroon belonged to the clan of Moses, but he oppressed them. We had given him treasures, the keys of which would weigh down a group of strong men. His people said to him, "Do not exult; God does not love the exultant.

77 But seek, with what God has given you, the Home of the Hereafter, and do not neglect your share of this world. And be charitable, as God has been charitable to you. And do not seek corruption in the land. God does not like the seekers of corruption."

78 He said, "I was given all this on account of knowledge I possess." Did he not know that God destroyed many generations before him, who were stronger than he, and possessed greater riches? But the guilty will not be asked about their sins.

79 And he went out before his people in his splendor. Those who desired the worldly life said, "If only we possessed the likes of what Quaroon was given. He is indeed very fortunate."

80 But those who were given knowledge said, "Woe to you! The reward of God is better for those who believe and do righteous deeds." Yet none attains it except the steadfast.

81 So We caused the earth to cave in on him and his mansion. He had no company to save him from God, and he could not defend himself.

82 Those who had wished they were in his position the day before were saying, "Indeed, it is God who spreads the bounty to whomever He wills of His servants, and restricts it. Had God not been gracious to us, He would have caved in on us. No wonder the ungrateful never prosper."

83 That Home of the Hereafter—We assign it for those who seek no superiority on earth, nor corruption. And the outcome is for the cautious.

84 Whoever brings a virtue will receive better than it. But whoever brings evil—the evildoers will be rewarded only according to what they used to do.

85 He Who ordained the Quran for you will return you Home. Say, "My Lord knows best who comes with guidance, and who is in manifest error."

86 You did not expect the Scripture to be transmitted to you, except as mercy from your Lord. Therefore, do not be a supporter of the disbelievers.

87 And do not let them divert you from God's revelations after they have been revealed to you. And pray to your Lord, and never be of the polytheists.

88 And do not invoke with God any other god. There is no god but He. All things perish, except His presence. His is the judgment, and to Him you will be returned.

Luqman (Luqman)

In the name of God, the Gracious, the Merciful.

1 Alif, Lam, Meem.

2 These are the Verses of the Wise Book.

3 A guide and a mercy for the righteous.

4 Those who observe the prayer, and pay the obligatory charity, and are certain of the Hereafter.

5 These are upon guidance from their Lord. These are the successful.

6 Among the people is he who trades in distracting tales; intending, without knowledge, to lead away from God's way, and to make a mockery of it. These will have a humiliating punishment.

7 And when Our Verses are recited to him, he turns away in pride, as though he did not hear them, as though there is deafness in his ears. So inform him of a painful punishment.

8 As for those who believe and do good deeds—for them are the Gardens of Bliss.

9 Dwelling therein forever. The promise of God is true. He is the Mighty, the Wise.

10 He created the heavens without pillars that you can see, and placed stabilizers on earth lest it shifts with you, and scattered throughout it all kinds of creatures. And from the sky We sent down water, and caused to grow therein of every noble pair.

11 Such is God's creation. Now show me what those besides Him have created. In fact, the wicked are in obvious error.

12 We endowed Luqman with wisdom: "Give thanks to God." Whoever is appreciative—is appreciative for the benefit of his own soul. And whoever is unappreciative—God is Sufficient and Praiseworthy.

13 When Luqman said to his son, as he advised him, "O my son, do not associate anything with God, for idolatry is a terrible wrong."

14 We have entrusted the human being with the care of his parents. His mother carried him through hardship upon hardship, weaning him in two years. So give thanks to Me, and to your parents. To Me is the destination.

15 But if they strive to have you associate with Me something of which you have no knowledge, do not obey them. But keep them company in this life, in kindness, and follow the path of him who turns to Me. Then to Me is your return; and I will inform you of what you used to do.

16 "O my son, even if it were the weight of a mustard-seed, in a rock, or in the heavens, or on earth, God will bring it to light. God is Kind and Expert.

17 O my son, observe the prayer, advocate righteousness, forbid evil, and be patient over what has befallen you. These are of the most honorable traits.

18 And do not treat people with arrogance, nor walk proudly on earth. God does not love the arrogant showoffs.

19 And moderate your stride, and lower your voice. The most repulsive of voices is the donkey's voice."

20 Do you not see how God placed at your service everything in the heavens and the earth? How He showered you with His blessings, both outward and inward? Yet among the people is he who argues about God without knowledge, without guidance, and without an enlightening Scripture.

21 And when it is said to them, "Follow what God has revealed," they say, "Rather, we follow what we found our parents devoted to." Even if Satan is calling them to the suffering of the Blaze?

22 Whoever submits himself wholly to God, and is a doer of good, has grasped the most trustworthy handle. With God rests the outcome of all events.

23 Whoever disbelieves—let not his disbelief sadden you. To Us is their return. Then We will inform them of what they did. God knows what lies within the hearts.

24 We give them a little comfort; then We compel them to a harsh torment.

25 And if you ask them, "Who created the heavens and the earth?" They will say, "God." Say, "Praise be to God." But most of them do not know.

26 To God belongs everything in the heavens and the earth. God is the Rich, the Praised.

27 If all the trees on earth were pens, filled by the ocean, with seven more oceans besides, the Words of God would not run out. God is Majestic and Wise.

28 Your creation and your resurrection are only as a single soul. God is Hearing and Seeing.

29 Have you not seen how God merges the night into the day, and merges the day into the night? That He subjected the sun and the moon, each running for a stated term? And that God is Cognizant of everything you do?

30 That is because God is the Reality, and what they worship besides Him is falsehood, and because God is the Exalted, the Supreme.

31 Have you not seen how the ships sail through the sea, by the grace of God, to show you of His wonders? In that are signs for every persevering, thankful person.

32 When waves, like canopies, cover them, they call upon God, devoting their religion to Him. But when He has delivered them to dry land, some of them waver. No one renounces Our revelations except the treacherous blasphemer.

33 O people! Be conscious of your Lord, and dread a Day when no parent can avail his child, nor can a child avail his parent, in anything. The promise of God is true. Therefore, do not let this life deceive you, nor let illusions deceive you regarding God.

34 With God rests the knowledge of the Hour. He sends down the rain, and He knows what the wombs contain. No soul knows what it will reap tomorrow, and no soul knows in what land it will die. God is All-Knowing, Well-Informed.

Prostration (as-Sajdah)

In the name of God, the Gracious, the Merciful.

1 Alif, Lam, Meem.

2 The revelation of the Book, without a doubt, is from the Lord of the Universe.

3 Yet they say, "He made it up." In fact, it is the Truth from your Lord, to warn a people who received no warner before you, that they may be guided.

4 God is He who created the heavens and the earth and everything between them in six days, and then established Himself on the Throne. Apart from Him, you have no master and no intercessor. Will you not reflect?

5 He regulates all affairs, from the heavens, to the earth. Then it ascends to Him on a Day the length of which is a thousand years by your count.

6 That is the Knower of the Invisible and the Visible, the Powerful, the Merciful.

7 He who perfected everything He created, and originated the creation of man from clay.

8 Then made his reproduction from an extract of an insignificant fluid.

9 Then He proportioned him, and breathed into him of His Spirit. Then He gave you the hearing, and the eyesight, and the brains—but rarely do you give thanks.

10 And they say, "When we are lost into the earth, shall we be in a new creation?" In fact, they deny the meeting with their Lord.

11 Say, "The angel of death put in charge of you will reclaim you. Then to your Lord you will be returned."

12 If only you could see the guilty, bowing their heads before their Lord: "Our Lord, we have seen and we have heard, so send us back, and we will act righteously; we are now convinced."

13 Had We willed, We could have given every soul its guidance, but the declaration from Me will come true: "I will fill Hell with jinn and humans, altogether."

14 So taste, because you forgot the meeting of this Day of yours; We have forgotten you; so taste the eternal torment for what you used to do.

15 They believe in Our communications, those who, when reminded of them, fall down prostrate, and glorify their Lord with praise, and are not proud.

16 Their sides shun their beds, as they pray to their Lord, out of reverence and hope; and from Our provisions to them, they give.

17 No soul knows what eye's delight awaits them—a reward for what they used to do.

18 Is someone who is faithful like someone who is a sinner? They are not equal.

19 As for those who believe and do righteous deeds, for them are the Gardens of Shelter—hospitality for what they used to do.

20 But as for those who transgressed, their shelter is the Fire. Every time they try to get out of it, they will be brought back into it, and it will be said to them, "Taste the suffering of the Fire which you used to deny."

21 We will make them taste the lesser torment, prior to the greater torment, so that they may return.

22 Who is more wrong than he, who, when reminded of his Lord's revelations, turns away from them? We will certainly wreak vengeance upon the criminals.

23 We gave Moses the Book; so do not be in doubt regarding His encounter; and We made it a guidance for the Children of Israel.

24 And We appointed leaders from among them, guiding by Our command, as long as they persevered and were certain of Our communications.

25 Your Lord will judge between them on the Day of Resurrection regarding everything they had disputed.

26 Is it not a lesson for them, how many generations We have destroyed before them, in whose habitations they walk? Surely in that are signs. Do they not hear?

27 Do they not see how We conduct the water to a dry land, and with it We produce vegetation, from which their livestock eat, and themselves? Do they not see?

28 And they say, "When is this victory, if you are truthful?"

29 Say, "On the day of victory, the faith of those who disbelieved will be of no avail to them, and they will not be granted respite."

30 So turn away from them, and wait. They too are waiting.

Originator (Fatir)

In the name of God, the Gracious, the Merciful.

1 Praise be to God, Originator of the heavens and the earth, Maker of the angels messengers with wings—double, triple, and quadruple. He adds to creation as He wills. God is Able to do all things.

2 Whatever mercy God unfolds for the people, none can withhold it. And if He withholds it, none can release it thereafter. He is the Exalted in Power, Full of Wisdom.

3 O people! Remember God's blessings upon you. Is there a creator other than God who provides for you from the heaven and the earth? There is no god but He. So how are you misled?

4 If they reject you, messengers before you were also rejected. To God all matters are returned.

5 O people! The promise of God is true; so let not the lowly life seduce you, and let not the Tempter tempt you away from God.

6 Satan is an enemy to you, so treat him as an enemy. He only invites his gang to be among the inmates of the Inferno.

7 Those who disbelieve will suffer a harsh punishment, but those who believe and do righteous deeds will have forgiveness and a great reward.

8 What of him whose evil deed was made attractive to him, and so he regards it as good? God leads astray whomever He wills, and He guides whomever He wills. Therefore, do not waste yourself sorrowing over them. God knows exactly what they do.

9 God is He who sends the winds, which agitate clouds, which We drive to a dead land, and thereby revive the ground after it had died. Likewise is the Resurrection.

10 Whoever desires honor—all honor belongs to God. To Him ascends speech that is pure, and He elevates righteous conduct. As for those who plot evil, a terrible punishment awaits them, and the planning of these will fail.

11 God created you from dust, then from a small drop; then He made you pairs. No female conceives, or delivers, except with His knowledge. No living thing advances in years, or its life is shortened, except it be in a Record. That is surely easy for God.

12 The two seas are not the same. One is fresh, sweet, good to drink, while the other is salty and bitter. Yet from each you eat tender meat, and extract jewelry which you wear. And you see the ships plowing through them, so that you may seek of His bounty, so that you may give thanks.

13 He merges the night into the day, and He merges the day into the night; and He regulates the sun and the moon, each running for a stated term. Such is God, your Lord; His is the sovereignty. As for those you call upon besides Him, they do not possess a speck.

14 If you pray to them, they cannot hear your prayer. And even if they heard, they would not answer you. And on the Day of Resurrection, they will reject your partnership. None informs you like an Expert.

15 O people! It is you who are the poor, in need of God; while God is the Rich, the Praiseworthy.

16 If He wills, He can do away with you, and produce a new creation.

17 And that would not be difficult for God.

18 No burdened soul can carry the burden of another. Even if one weighted down calls for help with its burden, nothing can be lifted from it, even if they were related. You are to warn those who fear their Lord inwardly, and perform the prayer. He who purifies himself purifies himself for his own good. To God is the ultimate return.

19 Not equal are the blind and the seeing.

20 Nor are the darkness and the light.

21 Nor are the shade and the torrid heat.

22 Nor are equal the living and the dead. God causes whomever He wills to hear, but you cannot make those in the graves hear.

23 You are only a warner.

24 We sent you with the truth; a bearer of good news, and a warner. There is no community but a warner has passed through it.

25 If they disbelieve you, those before them also disbelieved. Their messengers came to them with the clear proofs, with the Psalms, and with the Enlightening Scripture.

26 Then I seized those who disbelieved—so how was My rejection?

27 Have you not seen that God sends down water from the sky? With it We produce fruits of various colors. And in the mountains are streaks of white and red—varying in their hue—and pitch-black.

28 Likewise, human beings, animals, and livestock come in various colors. From among His servants, the learned fear God. God is Almighty, Oft-Forgiving.

29 Those who recite the Book of God, and perform the prayer, and spend of what We have provided for them, secretly and publicly, expect a trade that will not fail.

30 He will pay them their dues in full, and will increase them from His bounty. He is Forgiving and Appreciative.

31 What We inspired in you, of the Book, is the truth, confirming what preceded it. God is Well-Informed of His servants, All-Seeing.

32 Then We passed the Book to those of Our servants whom We chose. Some of them wrong their souls, and some follow a middle course, and some are in the foremost in good deeds by God's leave; that is the greatest blessing.

33 The Gardens of Eden, which they will enter. They will be adorned therein with gold bracelets and pearls, and their garments therein will be of silk.

34 And they will say, "Praise God, who has lifted all sorrow from us. Our Lord is Most Forgiving, Most Appreciative.

35 He Who settled us in the Home of Permanence, by His grace, where boredom will not touch us, and fatigue will not afflict us."

36 As for those who disbelieve, for them is the Fire of Hell, wherein they will never be finished off and die, nor will its punishment be lightened for them. Thus We will repay every ingrate.

37 And they will scream therein, "Our Lord, let us out, and we will act righteously, differently from the way we used to act." Did We not give you a life long enough, in which anyone who wanted to understand would have understood? And the warner did come to you. So taste. The evildoers will have no helper.

38 God is the Knower of the future of the heavens and the earth. He knows what the hearts contain.

39 It is He who made you successors on earth. Whoever disbelieves, his disbelief will recoil upon him. The disbelief of the disbelievers adds only to their Lord's disfavor of them. The disbelief of the disbelievers adds only to their perdition.

40 Say, "Have you considered those partners of yours that you worship instead of God? Show me what they have created on earth. Or do they have any share in the heavens?" Or have We given them a book whose clear teachings they follow? In fact, the wrongdoers promise one another nothing but delusions.

41 God holds the heavens and the earth, lest they fall apart. And were they to fall apart, there is none to hold them together except He. He is Most Clement, Most Forgiving.

42 And they swore by God with their solemn oaths, that if a warner came to them, they would be more guided than any other people. Yet when a warner came to them, it only increased them in aversion.

43 Priding themselves on earth, and scheming evil. But evil scheming overwhelms none but its authors. Do they expect anything but the precedent of the ancients? You will not find any change in God's practice, and you will not find any substitute to God's practice.

44 Have they not journeyed in the land and observed the fate of those who preceded them? They were superior to them in strength. But nothing can defeat God in the heavens or on Earth. He is indeed Omniscient and Omnipotent.

45 If God were to punish the people for what they have earned, He would not leave a single living creature on its surface. But He defers them until a stated time. Then, when their time has arrived—God is Observant of His creatures.

Ya-Seen (Ya-Seen)

In the name of God, the Gracious, the Merciful.

1 Ya, Seen.

2 By the Wise Quran.

3 You are one of the messengers.

4 On a straight path.

5 The revelation of the Almighty, the Merciful.

6 To warn a people whose ancestors were not warned, and so they are unaware.

7 The Word was realized against most of them, for they do not believe.

8 We placed shackles around their necks, up to their chins, so they are stiff-necked.

9 And We placed a barrier in front of them, and a barrier behind them, and We have enshrouded them, so they cannot see.

10 It is the same for them, whether you warn them, or do not warn them—they will not believe.

11 You warn only him who follows the Message, and fears the Most Gracious inwardly. So give him good news of forgiveness, and a generous reward.

12 It is We who revive the dead; and We write down what they have forwarded, and their traces. We have tallied all things in a Clear Record.

13 And cite for them the parable of the landlords of the town—when the messengers came to it.

14 We sent them two messengers, but they denied them both, so We reinforced them with a third. They said, "We are messengers to you."

15 They said, "You are nothing but humans like us, and the Gracious did not send down anything; you are only lying."

16 They said, "Our Lord knows that we are messengers to you.

17 And our only duty is clear communication."

18 They said, "We see an evil omen in you; if you do not give up, we will stone you, and a painful punishment from us will befall you."

19 They said, "Your evil omen is upon you. Is it because you were reminded? But you are an extravagant people."

20 Then a man came running from the remotest part of the city. He said, "O my people, follow the messengers.

21 Follow those who ask you of no wage, and are themselves guided.

22 "And why should I not worship Him Who created me, and to Whom you will be returned?

23 Shall I take other gods instead of Him? If the Merciful desires harm for me, their intercession will not avail me at all, nor will they save me.

24 In that case, I would be completely lost.

25 I have believed in your Lord, so listen to me."

26 It was said, "Enter Paradise." He said, "If only my people knew.

27 How my Lord has forgiven me, and made me one of the honored."

28 After him, We sent down no hosts from heaven to his people; nor would We ever send any down.

29 It was just one Cry, and they were stilled.

30 Alas for the servants. No messenger ever came to them, but they ridiculed him.

31 Have they not considered how many generations We destroyed before them; and that unto them they will not return?

32 All of them, every single one of them, will be arraigned before Us.

33 And there is a sign for them in the dead land: We give it life, and produce from it grains from which they eat.

34 And We place in it gardens of palm-trees and vines, and cause springs to gush out of it.

35 That they may eat from its fruits, although their hands did not make it. Will they not be appreciative?

36 Glory be to Him who created all the pairs; of what the earth produces, and of their own selves, and of what they do not know.

37 Another sign for them is the night: We strip the day out of it—and they are in darkness.

38 And the sun runs towards its destination. Such is the design of the Almighty, the All-Knowing.

39 And the moon: We have disposed it in phases, until it returns like the old twig.

40 The sun is not to overtake the moon, nor is the night to outpace the day. Each floats in an orbit.

41 Another sign for them is that We carried their offspring in the laden Ark.

42 And We created for them the like of it, in which they ride.

43 If We will, We can drown them—with no screaming to be heard from them, nor will they be saved.

44 Except by a mercy from Us, and enjoyment for a while.

45 Yet when it is said to them, "Beware of what lies before you, and what lies behind you, that you may receive mercy."

46 Yet never came to them a sign of their Lord's signs, but they turned away from it.

47 And when it is said to them, "Spend of what God has provided for you," those who disbelieve say to those who believe, "Shall we feed someone whom God could feed, if He so willed? You must be deeply misguided."

48 And they say, "When will this promise be, if you are truthful?"

49 All they can expect is a single blast, which will seize them while they feud.

50 They will not be able to make a will, nor will they return to their families.

51 The Trumpet will be blown, then behold, they will rush from the tombs to their Lord.

52 They will say, "Woe to us! Who resurrected us from our resting-place?" This is what the Most Gracious had promised, and the messengers have spoken the truth."

53 It will be but a single scream; and behold, they will all be brought before Us.

54 On that Day, no soul will be wronged in the least, and you will be recompensed only for what you used to do.

55 The inhabitants of Paradise, on that Day, will be happily busy.

56 They and their spouses, in shades, reclining on couches.

57 They will have therein fruits. They will have whatever they call for.

58 Peace—a saying from a Most Merciful Lord.

59 But step aside today, you criminals.

60 Did I not covenant with you, O Children of Adam, that you shall not serve the devil? That he is your sworn enemy?

61 And that you shall serve Me? This is a straight path.

62 He has misled a great multitude of you. Did you not understand?

63 This is Hellfire, which you were promised.

64 Roast in it today, because you persistently disbelieved.

65 On this Day, We will seal their mouths, and their hands will speak to Us, and their feet will testify to everything they had done.

66 If We will, We can blind their eyes as they rush towards the path—but how will they see?

67 And if We will, We can cripple them in their place; so they can neither move forward, nor go back.

68 Whomever We grant old age, We reverse his development. Do they not understand?

69 We did not teach him poetry, nor is it proper for him. It is only a reminder, and a Clear Quran.

70 That he may warn whoever is alive, and prove the Word against the faithless.

71 Have they not seen that We created for them, of Our Handiwork, livestock that they own?

72 And We subdued them for them. Some they ride, and some they eat.

73 And they have in them other benefits, and drinks. Will they not give thanks?

74 Yet they have taken to themselves gods other than God, that perhaps they may be helped.

75 They cannot help them, although they are arrayed as troops for them.

76 So let their words not sadden you. We know what they conceal, and what they reveal.

77 Does the human being not consider that We created him from a seed? Yet he becomes a fierce adversary.

78 And he produces arguments against Us, and he forgets his own creation. He says, "Who will revive the bones when they have decayed?"

79 Say, "He who initiated them in the first instance will revive them. He has knowledge of every creation."

80 He who produced fuel for you from the green trees, with which you kindle a fire.

81 Is not He who created the heavens and the earth able to create the like of them? Certainly. He is the Supreme All-Knowing Creator.

82 His command, when He wills a thing, is to say to it, "Be," and it comes to be.

83 So glory be to Him in whose hand is the dominion of everything, and to Him you will be returned.

Throngs (az-Zumar)

In the name of God, the Gracious, the Merciful.

1 The revelation of the Book is from God, the Mighty and Wise.

2 We sent down to you the Book with the truth, so serve God, devoting your religion to Him.

3 Is not to God that sincere faith is due? As for those who take guardians besides Him, "We only worship them that they may bring us nearer to God." God will judge between them regarding their differences. God does not guide the lying blasphemer.

4 If God wanted to have a son, He could have selected from His creation at will. Glory be to Him. He is God, the One, the Prevailing.

5 He created the heavens and the earth with reason. He wraps the night around the day, and He wraps the day around the night. And He regulates the sun and the moon, each running along a specific course. He is indeed the Almighty, the Forgiver.

6 He created you from one person, then made from it its mate, and brought down livestock for you—eight kinds in pairs. He creates you in the wombs of your mothers, in successive formations, in a triple darkness. Such is God, your Lord. His is the kingdom. There is no god but He. So what made you deviate?

7 If you disbelieve, God is Independent of you, yet He does not approve ingratitude on the part of His servants. And if you are thankful, He will approve that in you. No bearer of burden can bear the burden of another. Then to your Lord is your return; and He will inform you of what you used to do. He is aware of what the hearts contain.

8 When some adversity touches the human being, he prays to his Lord, repenting to Him. But then, when He confers on him a grace of His, he forgets what he was praying for before, and he attributes rivals to God, in order to lead astray from His way. Say, "Enjoy your disbelief for a little while; you will be among the inmates of the Fire."

9 Is he who worships devoutly during the watches of the night, prostrating himself and standing up, mindful of the Hereafter, and placing his hope in the mercy of his Lord? Say, "Are those who know and those who do not know equal?" Only those possessed of reason will remember.

10 Say, "O My devotees who have believed, keep your duty to your Lord. For those who do good in this world, is goodness. And God's earth is vast. The steadfast will be paid their wages in full, without reckoning."

11 Say, "I was commanded to serve God, devoting my religion exclusively to Him.

12 And I was commanded to be the first of those who submit."

13 Say, "I fear, if I disobeyed my Lord, the punishment of a horrendous Day."

14 Say, "It is God I worship, sincere in my faith in Him."

15 "But you can worship whatever you wish besides Him." Say, "The losers are those who lose their souls and their people on the Day of Resurrection." That is indeed the obvious loss.

16 They will have layers of Fire above them, and layers beneath them. That is how God strikes fear into His servants—"O My servants! Beware of Me!"

17 As for those who avoid the worship of idols, and devote themselves to God—theirs is the good news. So give good news to My servants.

18 Those who listen to the Word, and follow the best of it. These are they whom God has guided. These are they who possess intellect.

19 What about someone who has deserved the sentence of punishment? Is it you who can save those in the Fire?

20 But those who fear their Lord will have mansions upon mansions, built high, with streams flowing beneath them. The promise of God; and God never breaks a promise.

21 Have you not considered how God sends down water from the sky, then He makes it flow into underground wells, then He produces with it plants of various colors, then they wither and you see them yellowing, then He turns them into debris? Surely in this is a reminder for those with understanding.

22 What about someone whose heart God has opened to Islam, so that he follows a light from His Lord? Woe to those whose hearts are hardened against the mention of God. Those are in manifest error.

23 God has sent down the best of narrations: a Scripture consistent and paired. The skins of those who reverence their Lord shiver from it, then their skins and their hearts soften up to the remembrance of God. Such is God's guidance; He guides with it whomever He wills. But whomever God leaves astray, for him there is no guide.

24 What about someone who covers his face against the terrible misery of the Day of Resurrection? To the evildoers it will be said, "Taste what you used to earn."

25 Those before them also denied the truth, so the penalty came upon them from where they did not perceive.

26 God made them taste disgrace in the present life, but the punishment of the Hereafter is worse, if they only knew.

27 We have cited in this Quran for mankind every ideal, that they may take heed.

28 An Arabic Quran, without any defect, so they may become righteous.

29 God cites the example of a man shared by partners at odds, and a man belonging exclusively to one man. Are they equal in status? Praise be to God, but most of them do not know.

30 You will die, and they will die.

31 Then, on the Day of Resurrection, you will be quarrelling before your Lord.

32 Who is more evil than he who lies about God, and denies the truth when it has come to him? Is there not in Hell room for the ungrateful?

33 But he who promotes the truth, and testifies to it—these are the righteous.

34 They will have whatever they please with their Lord. Such is the reward for the virtuous.

35 God will acquit them of the worst of their deeds, and will reward them according to the best of what they used to do.

36 Is God not enough for His servant? And they frighten you with those besides Him. Whomever God sends astray, for him there is no guide.

37 And whomever God guides, for him there is no misleader. Is God not Powerful and Vengeful?

38 And if you asked them, "Who created the heavens and the earth?" they would say, "God." Say, "Have you seen those you pray to instead of God? If God willed any harm for me, can they lift His harm? And if He willed a blessing for me, can they hold back His mercy?" Say, "God suffices for me. On Him the reliant rely."

39 Say: "O my people, work according to your ability; and so will I. Then you will know.

40 Who will receive a humiliating punishment, and on whom will fall a lasting torment."

41 We sent down upon you the Book for mankind in truth. He who follows guidance does so for the good of his soul. And he who strays in error does so to its detriment. You are not their overseer.

42 God takes the souls at the time of their death, and those that have not died during their sleep. He retains those for which He has decreed death, and He releases the others until a predetermined time. In that are signs for people who reflect.

43 Or have they chosen intercessors other than God? Say, "Even though they have no power over anything, and are devoid of reason?"

44 Say, "All intercession is up to God. To Him belongs the kingdom of the heavens and the earth. Then to Him you will be returned."

45 When God alone is mentioned, the hearts of those who do not believe in the Hereafter shrink with resentment. But when those other than Him are mentioned, they become filled with joy.

46 Say, "Our God, Initiator of the heavens and the earth, Knower of all secrets and declarations. You will judge between your servants regarding what they had differed about."

47 If those who did wrong owned everything on earth, and the like of it with it, they would redeem themselves with it from the terrible suffering on the Day of Resurrection. But there will appear to them from God what they never anticipated.

48 There will appear to them the evils of their deeds, and they will be surrounded by what they used to ridicule.

49 When adversity touches the human being, he calls on Us. But then, when We favor him with a blessing from Us, he says, "I have attained this by virtue of my knowledge." However, it is a test, but most of them do not know.

50 Those before them said it, but what they had earned did not avail them.

51 The evils of their deeds caught up with them. And the wrongdoers among these will also be afflicted by the evils of what they earned, and they cannot prevent it.

52 Do they not know that God extends the provision to whomever He wills, and constricts it? In that are signs for people who believe.

53 Say, "O My servants who have transgressed against themselves: do not despair of God's mercy, for God forgives all sins. He is indeed the Forgiver, the Clement."

54 And turn to your Lord, and submit to Him, before the retribution comes upon you. Then you will not be helped.

55 And follow the best of what was revealed to you from your Lord, before the punishment comes upon you suddenly, while you are unaware.

56 So that a soul may not say, "How sorry I am, for having neglected my duty to God, and for having been of the scoffers."

57 Or say, "Had God guided me; I would have been of the pious."

58 Or say, when it sees the penalty, "If only I had another chance, I would be of the virtuous."

59 Yes indeed! My Verses did come to you, but you called them lies, turned arrogant, and were of the faithless.

60 On the Day of Resurrection, you will see those who told lies about God with their faces blackened. Is there not a place in Hell for the arrogant?

61 And God will save those who maintained righteousness to their place of salvation. No harm will touch them, nor will they grieve.

62 God is the Creator of all things, and He is in Charge of all things.

63 To Him belong the reins of the heavens and the earth. But those who blaspheme against the revelations of God—it is they who are the losers.

64 Say, "Is it other than God you instruct me to worship, you ignorant ones?"

65 It was revealed to you, and to those before you, that if you idolize, your works will be in vain, and you will be of the losers.

66 Rather, worship God, and be of the appreciative.

67 They have not esteemed God as He ought to be esteemed. The entire earth will be in His grip on the Day of Resurrection, and the heavens will be folded in His right. Immaculate is He, and Transcendent He is beyond the associations they make.

68 And the Trumpet will be sounded, whereupon everyone in the heavens and the earth will be stunned, except whomever God wills. Then it will be sounded another time, whereupon they will rise up, looking on.

69 And the earth will shine with the Light of its Lord; and the Book will be put in place; and the prophets and the witnesses will be brought in; and Judgment will be passed among them equitably, and they will not be wronged.

70 And every soul will be fully compensated for what it had done. He is well aware of what they do.

71 Those who disbelieved will be driven to Hell in throngs. Until, when they have reached it, and its gates are opened, its keepers will say to them, "Did not messengers from among you come to you, reciting to you the revelations of your Lord, and warning you of the meeting of this Day of yours?" They will say, "Yes, but the verdict of punishment is justified against the disbelievers."

72 It will be said, "Enter the gates of Hell, to abide therein eternally." How wretched is the destination of the arrogant.

73 And those who feared their Lord will be led to Paradise in throngs. Until, when they have reached it, and its gates are opened, its keepers will say to them, "Peace be upon you, you have been good, so enter it, to abide therein eternally."

74 And they will say, "Praise be to God, who has fulfilled His promise to us, and made us inherit the land, enjoying Paradise as we please." How excellent is the reward of the workers.

75 And you will see the angels hovering around the Throne, glorifying their Lord with praise. And it will be judged between them equitably, and it will be said, "Praise be to God, Lord of the Worlds."

Detailed (Fussilat)

In the name of God, the Gracious, the Merciful.

1 Ha, Meem.

2 A revelation from the Most Gracious, the Most Merciful.

3 A Scripture whose Verses are detailed, a Quran in Arabic for people who know.

4 Bringing good news, and giving warnings. But most of them turn away, so they do not listen.

5 And they say, "Our hearts are screened from what you call us to, and in our ears is deafness, and between us and you is a barrier. So do what you want, and so will we."

6 Say, "I am only a human like you; it is inspired in me that your God is One God. So be upright towards Him, and seek forgiveness from Him." And woe to the idolaters.

7 Those who do not pay the alms; and regarding the Hereafter, they are disbelievers.

8 As for those who believe and do righteous deeds—for them is a reward uninterrupted.

9 Say, "Do you reject the One who created the earth in two days? And you attribute equals to Him? That is the Lord of the Universe."

10 He placed stabilizers over it; and blessed it; and planned its provisions in four days, equally to the seekers.

11 Then He turned to the sky, and it was smoke, and said to it and to the earth, "Come, willingly or unwillingly." They said, "We come willingly."

12 So He completed them as seven universes in two days, and He assigned to each universe its laws. And We decorated the lower universe with lamps, and for protection. That is the design of the Almighty, the All-Knowing.

13 But if they turn away, say, "I have warned you of a thunderbolt, like the thunderbolt of Aad and Thamood."

14 Their messengers came to them, from before them and from behind them, saying, "Do not worship anyone but God." They said, "Had our Lord willed, He would have sent down angels; Therefore, we reject what you are sent with."

15 As for Aad, they turned arrogant on earth, and opposed justice, and said, "Who is more powerful than us?" Have they not considered that God, who created them, is more powerful than they? And they went on denying Our revelations.

16 So We unleashed upon them a screaming wind, for a few miserable days, to make them taste the punishment of shame in this life; but the punishment of the Hereafter is more shameful; and they will not be saved.

17 And as for Thamood, We guided them, but they preferred blindness over guidance. So the thunderbolt of the humiliating punishment seized them, because of what they used to earn.

18 And We saved those who believed and were righteous.

19 The Day when God's enemies are herded into the Fire, forcibly.

20 Until, when they have reached it, their hearing, and their sight, and their skins will testify against them regarding what they used to do.

21 And they will say to their skins, "Why did you testify against us?" They will say, "God, Who made all things speak, made us speak. It is He who created you the first time, and to Him you are returned."

22 You were unable to hide yourselves from your hearing, and your sight, and your skins, to prevent them from testifying against you, and you imagined that God was unaware of much of what you do.

23 It is that thought of yours about your Lord that led you to ruin—so you became of the losers.

24 If they endure patiently, the Fire will be their residence; and if they make up excuses, they will not be pardoned.

25 We had assigned companions for them, who glamorized to them what was in front of them, and what was behind them. And the Word proved true against them in communities of jinn and humans that have passed away before them. They were losers.

26 Those who disbelieve say, "Do not listen to this Quran, and talk over it, so that you may prevail."

27 We will make those who disbelieve taste an intense agony, and We will recompense them according to the worst of what they used to do.

28 Such is the recompense of God's enemies—the Fire—where they will have their permanent home, in recompense for having disregarded Our revelations.

29 Those who disbelieved will say, "Our Lord, show us those who led us astray—among jinn and humans—and we will trample them under our feet, so they become of the lowest."

30 Surely, those who say: "Our Lord is God," and then go straight, the angels will descend upon them: "Do not fear, and do not grieve, but rejoice in the news of the Garden which you were promised.

31 We are your allies in this life and in the Hereafter, wherein you will have whatever your souls desire, and you will have therein whatever you call for.

32 As Hospitality from an All-Forgiving, Merciful One."

33 And who is better in speech than someone who calls to God, and acts with integrity, and says, "I am of those who submit"?

34 Good and evil are not equal. Repel evil with good, and the person who was your enemy becomes like an intimate friend.

35 But none will attain it except those who persevere, and none will attain it except the very fortunate.

36 When a temptation from the Devil provokes you, seek refuge in God; He is the Hearer, the Knower.

37 And of His signs are the night and the day, and the sun and the moon. Do not bow down to the sun, nor to the moon, but bow down to God, Who created them both, if it is Him that you serve.

38 But if they are too proud—those in the presence of your Lord praise Him night and day, and without ever tiring.

39 And of His signs is that you see the land still. But when We send down water upon it, it stirs and grows. Surely, He Who revived it will revive the dead. He is Able to do all things.

40 Those who despise Our revelations are not hidden from Us. Is he who is hurled into the Fire better? Or he who arrives safely on the Day of Resurrection? Do as you please; He is Seeing of everything you do.

41 Those who reject the Reminder when it has come to them—it is an invincible Book.

42 Falsehood cannot approach it, from before it or behind it. It is a revelation from One Wise and Praiseworthy.

43 Nothing is said to you but was said to the Messengers before you: your Lord is Possessor of Forgiveness, and Possessor of Painful Repayment.

44 Had We made it a Quran in a foreign language, they would have said, "If only its verses were made clear." Non-Arabic and an Arab? Say, "For those who believe, it is guidance and healing. But as for those who do not believe: there is heaviness in their ears, and it is blindness for them. These are being called from a distant place."

45 We gave Moses the Book, but disputes arose concerning it. Were it not for a prior decree from your Lord, judgment would have been pronounced between them. But they are in perplexing doubt concerning it.

46 Whoever acts righteously does so for himself; and whoever works evil does so against himself. Your Lord is not unjust to the servants.

47 To Him is referred the knowledge of the Hour. No fruit emerges from its sheath, and no female conceives or delivers, except with His knowledge. And on the Day when He calls out to them, "Where are My associates?" They will say, "We admit to you, none of us is a witness."

48 What they used to pray to before will forsake them, and they will realize that they have no escape.

49 The human being never tires of praying for good things; but when adversity afflicts him, he despairs and loses hope.

50 And when We let him taste a mercy from Us, after the adversity that had afflicted him, he will say, "This is mine, and I do not think that the Hour is coming; and even if I am returned to my Lord, I will have the very best with Him." We will inform those who disbelieve of what they did, and We will make them taste an awful punishment.

51 When We provide comfort for the human being, he withdraws and distances himself; but when adversity befalls him, he starts lengthy prayers.

52 Say, "Have you considered? If it is from God and you reject it—who is further astray than he who is cutoff and alienated?"

53 We will show them Our proofs on the horizons, and in their very souls, until it becomes clear to them that it is the truth. Is it not sufficient that your Lord is witness over everything?

54 Surely they are in doubt about the encounter with their Lord. Surely He comprehends everything.

Kneeling (al-Jathiyah)

In the name of God, the Gracious, the Merciful.

1 Ha, Meem.

2 The revelation of the Book is from God, the Exalted in Might, the Wise.

3 In the heavens and the earth are proofs for the believers.

4 And in your own creation, and in the creatures He scattered, are signs for people of firm faith.

5 And in the alternation of night and day, and in the sustenance God sends down from the sky, with which He revives the earth after its death, and in the circulation of the winds, are marvels for people who reason.

6 These are God's Verses which We recite to you in truth. In which message, after God and His revelations, will they believe?

7 Woe to every sinful liar.

8 Who hears God's revelations being recited to him, yet he persists arrogantly, as though he did not hear them. Announce to him a painful punishment.

9 And when he learns something of Our revelations, he takes them in mockery. For such there is a shameful punishment.

10 Beyond them lies Hell. What they have earned will not benefit them at all, nor will those they adopted as lords instead of God. They will have a terrible punishment.

11 This is guidance. Those who blaspheme their Lord's revelations will have a punishment of agonizing pain.

12 It is God who placed the sea at your service, so that ships may run through it by His command, and that you may seek of His bounty, and that you may give thanks.

13 And He placed at your service whatever is in the heavens and whatever is on earth—all is from Him. In that are signs for a people who think.

14 Tell those who believe to forgive those who do not hope for the Days of God. He will fully recompense people for whatever they have earned.

15 Whoever does a good deed, it is for his soul; and whoever commits evil, it is against it; then to your Lord you will be returned.

16 We gave the Children of Israel the Book, and wisdom, and prophecy; and We provided them with the good things; and We gave them advantage over all other people.

17 And We gave them precise rulings. They fell into dispute only after knowledge came to them, out of mutual rivalry. Your Lord will judge between them on the Day of Resurrection regarding the things they differed about.

18 Then We set you upon a pathway of faith, so follow it, and do not follow the inclinations of those who do not know.

19 They will not help you against God in any way. The wrongdoers are allies of one another, while God is the Protector of the righteous.

20 This is an illumination for mankind, and guidance, and mercy for people who believe with certainty.

21 Do those who perpetrate the evil deeds assume that We will regard them as equal to those who believe and do righteous deeds, whether in their life or their death? Evil is their judgment!

22 God created the heavens and the earth with justice, so that every soul will be repaid for what it has earned. And they will not be wronged.

23 Have you considered him who has taken his desire for his god? God has knowingly led him astray, and has sealed his hearing and his heart, and has placed a veil over his vision. Who will guide him after God? Will you not reflect?

24 And they say, "There is nothing but this our present life; we die and we live, and nothing destroys us except time." But they have no knowledge of that; they are only guessing.

25 When Our clarifying Verses are recited to them, their only argument is to say, "Bring back our ancestors, if you are truthful."

26 Say, "God gives you life, then He makes you die; then He gathers you for the Day of Resurrection, about which there is no doubt. But most people do not know."

27 To God belongs the kingship of the heavens and the earth. On the Day when the Hour takes place, on that Day the falsifiers will lose.

28 You will see every community on its knees; every community will be called to its Book: "Today you are being repaid for what you used to do.

29 This Book of Ours speaks about you in truth. We have been transcribing what you have been doing."

30 As for those who believed and did righteous deeds, their Lord will admit them into His mercy. That is the clear triumph.

31 But as for those who disbelieved: "Were My revelations not recited to you? But you turned arrogant, and were guilty people."

32 And when it was said, "The promise of God is true, and of the Hour there is no doubt," you said, "We do not know what the Hour is; we think it is only speculation; we are not convinced."

33 The evils of what they did will become evident to them, and the very thing they ridiculed will haunt them.

34 And it will be said, "Today We forget you, as you forgot the encounter of this Day of yours. Your abode is the Fire, and there are no saviors for you.

35 That is because you took God's revelations for a joke, and the worldly life lured you." So today they will not be brought out of it, and they will not be allowed to repent.

36 Praise belongs to God; Lord of the heavens, Lord of the earth, Lord of humanity.

37 To Him belongs all supremacy in the heavens and the earth. He is the Majestic, the Wise.

The Dunes (al-Ahqaf)

In the name of God, the Gracious, the Merciful.

1 Ha, Meem.

2 The sending down of the Scripture is from God, the Honorable, the Wise.

3 We did not create the heavens and the earth and what lies between them except with reason, and for a finite period. But the blasphemers continue to ignore the warnings they receive.

4 Say, "Have you considered those you worship instead of God? Show me which portion of the earth they have created. Or do they own a share of the heavens? Bring me a scripture prior to this one, or some trace of knowledge, if you are truthful."

5 Who is more wrong than him who invokes, besides God, those who will not answer him until the Day of Resurrection, and are heedless of their prayers?

6 And when humanity is gathered, they will be enemies to them, and will renounce their worship of them.

7 When Our revelations are recited to them, plain and clear, those who disbelieve say of the truth when it has come to them, "This is obviously magic."

8 Or do they say, "He invented it himself"? Say, "If I invented it myself, there is nothing you can do to protect me from God. He knows well what you are engaged in. He is sufficient witness between me and you. He is the Forgiver, the Merciful."

9 Say, "I am not different from the other messengers; and I do not know what will be done with me, or with you. I only follow what is inspired in me, and I am only a clear warner."

10 Say, "Have you considered? What if it is from God and you disbelieve in it? A witness from the Children of Israel testified to its like, and has believed, while you turned arrogant. God does not guide the unjust people."

11 Those who disbelieve say to those who believe, "If it were anything good, they would not have preceded us to it." And since they were not guided by it, they will say, "This is an ancient lie."

12 And before it was the Book of Moses, a model and a mercy. And this is a confirming Book, in the Arabic language, to warn those who do wrong—and good news for the doers of good.

13 Those who say, "Our Lord is God," then lead a righteous life—they have nothing to fear, nor shall they grieve.

14 These are the inhabitants of Paradise, where they will dwell forever—a reward for what they used to do.

15 We have enjoined upon man kindness to his parents. His mother carried him with difficulty, and delivered him with difficulty. His bearing and weaning takes thirty months. Until, when he has attained his maturity, and has reached forty years, he says, "Lord, enable me to appreciate the blessings You have bestowed upon me and upon my parents, and to act with righteousness, pleasing You. And improve my children for me. I have sincerely repented to You, and I am of those who have surrendered."

16 Those are they from whom We accept the best of their deeds, and We overlook their misdeeds, among the dwellers of Paradise—the promise of truth which they are promised.

17 As for him who says to his parents, "Enough of you! Are you promising me that I will be raised up, when generations have passed away before me?" While they cry for God's help, "Woe to you! Believe! The promise of God is true!" But he says, "These are nothing but tales of the ancients."

18 Those are they upon whom the sentence is justified, among the communities that have passed away before them, of jinn and humans. They are truly losers.

19 There are degrees for everyone, according to what they have done, and He will repay them for their works in full, and they will not be wronged.

20 On the Day when the faithless will be paraded before the Fire: "You have squandered your good in your worldly life, and you took pleasure in them. So today you are being repaid with the torment of shame, because of your unjust arrogance on earth, and because you used to sin."

21 And mention the brother of Aad, as he warned his people at the dunes. Warnings have passed away before him, and after him: "Worship none but God; I fear for you the punishment of a tremendous Day."

22 They said, "Did you come to us to divert us from our gods? Then bring us what you threaten us with, if you are being truthful."

23 He said, "The knowledge is only with God, and I inform you of what I was sent with; but I see you are an ignorant people."

24 Then, when they saw a cloud approaching their valley, they said, "This is a cloud that will bring us rain." "In fact, it is what you were impatient for: a wind in which is grievous suffering."

25 It will destroy everything by the command of its Lord. And when the morning came upon them, there was nothing to be seen except their dwellings. Thus We requite the guilty people.

26 We had empowered them in the same way as We empowered you; and We gave them the hearing, and the sight, and the minds. But neither their hearing, nor their sight, nor their minds availed them in any way. That is because they disregarded the revelations of God; and so they became surrounded by what they used to ridicule.

27 We have destroyed many townships around you, and diversified the signs, so that they may return.

28 Why then did the idols, whom they worshiped as means of nearness to God, not help them? In fact, they abandoned them. It was their lie, a fabrication of their own making.

29 Recall when We dispatched towards you a number of jinn, to listen to the Quran. When they came in its presence, they said, "Pay attention!" Then, when it was concluded, they rushed to their people, warning them.

30 They said, "O our people, we have heard a Scripture, sent down after Moses, confirming what came before it. It guides to the truth, and to a straight path.

31 O our people! Answer the caller to God, and believe in Him; and He will forgive you your sins, and will save you from a painful punishment."

32 He who does not answer the caller to God will not escape on earth, and has no protectors besides Him. Those are in obvious error.

33 Do they not realize that God, who created the heavens and the earth, and was never tired by creating them, is Able to revive the dead? Yes indeed; He is Capable of everything.

34 On the Day when those who disbelieved are presented to the Fire: "Is this not real?" They will say, "Yes, indeed, by our Lord." He will say, "Then taste the suffering for having disbelieved."

35 So be patient, as the messengers with resolve were patient, and do not be hasty regarding them. On the Day when they witness what they are promised, it will seem as if they had lasted only for an hour of a day. A proclamation: Will any be destroyed except the sinful people?

Muhammad (Muhammad)

In the name of God, the Gracious, the Merciful.

1 Those who disbelieve and repel from the path of God—He nullifies their works.

2 While those who believe, and work righteousness, and believe in what was sent down to Muhammad—and it is the truth from their Lord—He remits their sins, and relieves their concerns.

3 That is because those who disbelieve follow falsehoods, while those who believe follow the truth from their Lord. God thus cites for the people their examples.

4 When you encounter those who disbelieve, strike at their necks. Then, when you have routed them, bind them firmly. Then, either release them by grace, or by ransom, until war lays down its burdens. Had God willed, He could have defeated them Himself, but He thus tests some of you by means of others. As for those who are killed in the way of God, He will not let their deeds go to waste.

5 He will guide them, and will improve their state of mind.

6 And will admit them into Paradise, which He has identified for them.

7 O you who believe! If you support God, He will support you, and will strengthen your foothold.

8 But as for those who disbelieve, for them is perdition, and He will waste their deeds.

9 That is because they hated what God revealed, so He nullified their deeds.

10 Have they not journeyed through the earth and seen the consequences for those before them? God poured destruction upon them, and for the unbelievers is something comparable.

11 That is because God is the Master of those who believe, while the disbelievers have no master.

12 God will admit those who believe and do good deeds into gardens beneath which rivers flow. As for those who disbelieve, they enjoy themselves, and eat as cattle eat, and the Fire will be their dwelling.

13 How many a town was more powerful than your town which evicted you? We destroyed them, and there was no helper for them.

14 Is he who stands upon evidence from his Lord, like someone whose evil deed is made to appear good to him? And they follow their own desires?

15 The likeness of the Garden promised to the righteous: in it are rivers of pure water, and rivers of milk forever fresh, and rivers of wine delightful to the drinkers, and rivers of strained honey. And therein they will have of every fruit, and forgiveness from their Lord. Like one abiding in the Fire forever, and are given to drink boiling water, that cuts-up their bowels?

16 Among them are those who listen to you, but when they leave your presence, they say to those given knowledge, "What did he say just now?" Those are they whose hearts God has sealed, and they follow their own desires.

17 As for those who are guided, He increases them in guidance, and He has granted them their righteousness.

18 Are they just waiting until the Hour comes to them suddenly? Its tokens have already come. But how will they be reminded when it has come to them?

19 Know that there is no god but God, and ask forgiveness for your sin, and for the believing men and believing women. God knows your movements, and your resting-place.

20 Those who believe say, "If only a chapter is sent down." Yet when a decisive chapter is sent down, and fighting is mentioned in it, you see those in whose hearts is sickness looking at you with the look of someone fainting at death. So woe to them!

21 Obedience and upright speech. Then, when the matter is settled, being true to God would have been better for them.

22 If you turn away, you are likely to make mischief on earth, and sever your family ties.

23 Those are they whom God has cursed. He made them deaf, and blinded their sight.

24 Will they not ponder the Quran? Or are there locks upon their hearts?

25 Those who reverted after the guidance became clear to them—Satan has enticed them, and has given them latitude.

26 That is because they said to those who hated what God has revealed, "We will obey you in certain matters." But God knows their secret thoughts.

27 How about when the angels take them at death, beating their faces and their backs?

28 That is because they pursued what displeases God, and they disliked His approval, so He nullified their works.

29 Do those in whose hearts is sickness think that God will not expose their malice?

30 Had We willed, We could have shown them to you, and you would have recognized them by their marks. Yet you will recognize them by their tone of speech. And God knows your actions.

31 We will certainly test you, until We know those among you who strive, and those who are steadfast, and We will test your reactions.

32 Those who disbelieve, and hinder from the path of God, and oppose the Messenger after guidance has become clear to them—they will not hurt God in the least, but He will nullify their deeds.

33 O you who believe! Obey God, and obey the Messenger, and do not let your deeds go to waste.

34 Those who disbelieve, and hinder from God's path, and then die as disbelievers—God will not forgive them.

35 So do not waver and call for peace while you have the upper hand. God is with you, and He will not waste your efforts.

36 The life of this world is nothing but play and pastime. But if you have faith and lead a righteous life, He will grant you your rewards, and He will not ask you for your possessions.

37 Were He to ask you for it, and press you, you would become tightfisted, and He would expose your unwillingness.

38 Here you are, being called to spend in the cause of God. Among you are those who withhold; but whoever withholds is withholding against his own

soul. God is the Rich, while you are the needy. And if you turn away, He will replace you with another people, and they will not be like you.

Victory (al-Fath)

In the name of God, the Gracious, the Merciful.

1 We have granted you a conspicuous victory.

2 That God may forgive you your sin, past and to come, and complete His favors upon you, and guide you in a straight path.

3 And help you with an unwavering support.

4 It is He who sent down tranquility into the hearts of the believers, to add faith to their faith. To God belong the forces of the heavens and the earth. God is Knowing and Wise.

5 He will admit the believers, male and female, into Gardens beneath which rivers flow, to abide therein forever, and He will remit their sins. That, with God, is a great triumph.

6 And He will punish the hypocrites, male and female, and the idolaters, male and female, those who harbor evil thoughts about God. They are surrounded by evil; and God is angry with them, and has cursed them, and has prepared for them Hell—a miserable destination.

7 To God belong the troops of the heavens and the earth. God is Mighty and Wise.

8 We sent you as a witness, and a bearer of good news, and a warner.

9 That you may believe in God and His Messenger, and support Him, and honor Him, and praise Him morning and evening.

10 Those who pledge allegiance to you are pledging allegiance to God. The hand of God is over their hands. Whoever breaks his pledge breaks it to his own loss. And whoever fulfills his covenant with God, He will grant him a great reward.

11 The Desert-Arabs who remained behind will say to you, "Our belongings and our families have preoccupied us, so ask forgiveness for us." They say with their tongues what is not in their hearts. Say, "Who can avail you anything against God, if He desires loss for you, or desires gain for you?" In fact, God is Informed of what you do.

12 But you thought that the Messenger and the believers will never return to their families, and this seemed fine to your hearts; and you harbored evil thoughts, and were uncivilized people.

13 He who does not believe in God and His Messenger—We have prepared for the disbelievers a Blazing Fire.

14 To God belongs the kingdom of the heavens and the earth. He forgives whomever He wills, and He punishes whomever He wills. God is Forgiving and Merciful.

15 Those who lagged behind will say when you depart to collect the gains, "Let us follow you." They want to change the Word of God. Say, "You will not follow us; God has said so before." Then they will say, "But you are jealous of us." In fact, they understand only a little.

16 Say to the Desert-Arabs who lagged behind, "You will be called against a people of great might; you will fight them, unless they submit. If you obey, God will give you a fine reward. But if you turn away, as you turned away before, He will punish you with a painful punishment."

17 There is no blame on the blind, nor any blame on the lame, nor any blame on the sick. Whoever obeys God and His Messenger—He will admit him into gardens beneath which rivers flow; but whoever turns away—He will punish him with a painful punishment.

18 God was pleased with the believers, when they pledged allegiance to you under the tree. He knew what was in their hearts, and sent down serenity upon them, and rewarded them with an imminent conquest.

19 And abundant gains for them to capture. God is Mighty and Wise.

20 God has promised you abundant gains, which you will capture. He has expedited this for you, and has restrained people's hands from you; that it may be a sign to the believers, and that He may guide you on a straight path.

21 And other things, of which you were incapable, but God has encompassed them. God is Capable of everything.

22 If those who disbelieve had fought you, they would have turned back and fled, then found neither protector nor helper.

23 It is God's pattern, ongoing since the past. You will never find any change in God's pattern.

24 It is He who withheld their hands from you, and your hands from them, in the valley of Mecca, after giving you advantage over them. God is Observer of what you do.

25 It is they who disbelieved, and barred you from the Sacred Mosque, and prevented the offering from reaching its destination. Were it not for faithful men and faithful women, whom you did not know, you were about to hurt them, and became guilty of an unintentional crime. Thus God admits into His mercy whomever He wills. Had they dispersed, We would have punished those who disbelieved among them with a painful penalty.

26 Those who disbelieved filled their hearts with rage—the rage of the days of ignorance. But God sent His serenity down upon His Messenger, and upon the believers, and imposed on them the words of righteousness—of which they were most worthy and deserving. God is aware of everything.

27 God has fulfilled His Messenger's vision in truth: "You will enter the Sacred Mosque, God willing, in security, heads shaven, or hair cut short, not fearing. He knew what you did not know, and has granted besides that an imminent victory."

28 It is He who sent His Messenger with the guidance and the religion of truth, to make it prevail over all religions. God suffices as Witness.

29 Muhammad is the Messenger of God. Those with him are stern against the disbelievers, yet compassionate amongst themselves. You see them kneeling, prostrating, seeking blessings from God and approval. Their marks are on their faces from the effects of prostration. Such is their description in the Torah, and their description in the Gospel: like a plant that sprouts, becomes strong, grows thick, and rests on its stem, impressing the farmers. Through them He enrages the disbelievers. God has promised those among them who believe and do good deeds forgiveness and a great reward.

Qaf (Qaf)

In the name of God, the Gracious, the Merciful.

1 Qaf. By the Glorious Quran.

2 They marveled that a warner has come to them from among them. The disbelievers say, "This is something strange.

3 When we have died and become dust? This is a farfetched return."

4 We know what the earth consumes of them, and with Us is a comprehensive book.

5 But they denied the truth when it has come to them, so they are in a confused state.

6 Have they not observed the sky above them, how We constructed it, and decorated it, and it has no cracks?

7 And the earth, how We spread it out, and set on it mountains, and grew in it all kinds of delightful pairs?

8 A lesson and a reminder for every penitent worshiper.

9 And We brought down from the sky blessed water, and produced with it gardens and grain to harvest.

10 And the soaring palm trees, with clustered dates.

11 As sustenance for the servants. And We revive thereby a dead town. Likewise is the resurrection.

12 Before them the people of Noah denied the truth, and so did the dwellers of Russ, and Thamood.

13 And Aad, and Pharaoh, and the brethren of Lot.

14 And the Dwellers of the Woods, and the people of Tubba. They all rejected the messengers, so My threat came true.

15 Were We fatigued by the first creation? But they are in doubt of a new creation.

16 We created the human being, and We know what his soul whispers to him. We are nearer to him than his jugular vein.

17 As the two receivers receive, seated to the right and to the left.

18 Not a word does he utter, but there is a watcher by him, ready.

19 The daze of death has come in truth: "This is what you tried to evade."

20 And the Trumpet is blown: "This is the Promised Day."

21 And every soul will come forward, accompanied by a driver and a witness.

22 "You were in neglect of this, so We lifted your screen from you, and your vision today is keen."

23 And His escort will say, "This is what I have ready with me."

24 "Throw into Hell every stubborn disbeliever.

25 Preventer of good, aggressor, doubter.

26 Who fabricated another god with God; toss him into the intense agony."

27 His escort will say, "Our Lord, I did not make him rebel, but he was far astray."

28 He will say, "Do not feud in My presence—I had warned you in advance.

29 The decree from Me will not be changed, and I am not unjust to the servants."

30 On the Day when We will say to Hell, "Are you full?" And it will say, "Are there any more?"

31 And Paradise will be brought closer to the pious, not far away.

32 "This is what you were promised—for every careful penitent.

33 Who inwardly feared the Most Gracious, and came with a repentant heart.

34 Enter it in peace. This is the Day of Eternity."

35 Therein they will have whatever they desire—and We have even more.

36 How many generations before them, who were more powerful than they, did We destroy? They explored the lands—was there any escape?

37 In that is a reminder for whoever possesses a heart, or cares to listen and witness.

38 We created the heavens and the earth and what is between them in six days, and no fatigue touched Us.

39 So endure what they say, and proclaim the praises of your Lord before the rising of the sun, and before sunset.

40 And glorify Him during the night, and at the end of devotions.

41 And listen for the Day when the caller calls from a nearby place.

42 The Day when they will hear the Shout in all truth. That is the Day of Emergence.

43 It is We who control life and death, and to Us is the destination.

44 The Day when the earth will crack for them at once. That is an easy gathering for Us.

45 We are fully aware of what they say, and you are not a dictator over them. So remind by the Quran whoever fears My warning.

The Compassionate (ar-Rahman)

In the name of God, the Gracious, the Merciful.

1 The Compassionate.
2 Has taught the Quran.
3 He created man.
4 And taught him clear expression.
5 The sun and the moon move according to plan.
6 And the stars and the trees prostrate themselves.
7 And the sky, He raised; and He set up the balance.
8 So do not transgress in the balance.
9 But maintain the weights with justice, and do not violate the balance.
10 And the earth; He set up for the creatures.
11 In it are fruits, and palms in clusters.
12 And grains in the blades, and fragrant plants.
13 So which of your Lord's marvels will you deny?
14 He created man from hard clay, like bricks.
15 And created the jinn from a fusion of fire.
16 So which of your Lord's marvels will you deny?
17 Lord of the two Easts and Lord of the two Wests.
18 So which of your Lord's marvels will you deny?
19 He merged the two seas, converging together.
20 Between them is a barrier, which they do not overrun.
21 So which of your Lord's marvels will you deny?
22 From them emerge pearls and coral.
23 So which of your Lord's marvels will you deny?
24 His are the ships, raised above the sea like landmarks.
25 So which of your Lord's marvels will you deny?
26 Everyone upon it is perishing.
27 But will remain the Presence of your Lord, Full of Majesty and Splendor.
28 So which of your Lord's marvels will you deny?

29 Everyone in the heavens and the earth asks Him. Every day He is managing.

30 So which of your Lord's marvels will you deny?

31 We will attend to you, O prominent two.

32 So which of your Lord's marvels will you deny?

33 O society of jinn and humans! If you can pass through the bounds of the heavens and the earth, go ahead and pass. But you will not pass except with authorization.

34 So which of your Lord's marvels will you deny?

35 You will be bombarded with flares of fire and brass, and you will not succeed.

36 So which of your Lord's marvels will you deny?

37 When the sky splits apart, and becomes rose, like paint.

38 So which of your Lord's marvels will you deny?

39 On that Day, no human and no jinn will be asked about his sins.

40 So which of your Lord's marvels will you deny?

41 The guilty will be recognized by their marks; they will be taken by the forelocks and the feet.

42 So which of your Lord's marvels will you deny?

43 This is Hell that the guilty denied.

44 They circulate between it and between a seething bath.

45 So which of your Lord's marvels will you deny?

46 But for him who feared the standing of his Lord are two gardens.

47 So which of your Lord's marvels will you deny?

48 Full of varieties.

49 So which of your Lord's marvels will you deny?

50 In them are two flowing springs.

51 So which of your Lord's marvels will you deny?

52 In them are fruits of every kind, in pairs.

53 So which of your Lord's marvels will you deny?

54 Reclining on furnishings lined with brocade, and the fruits of the two gardens are near at hand.

55 So which of your Lord's marvels will you deny?

56 In them are maidens restraining their glances, untouched before by any man or jinn.

57 So which of your Lord's marvels will you deny?

58 As though they were rubies and corals.

59 So which of your Lord's marvels will you deny?

60 Is the reward of goodness anything but goodness?

61 So which of your Lord's marvels will you deny?

62 And beneath them are two gardens.

63 So which of your Lord's marvels will you deny?

64 Deep green.

65 So which of your Lord's marvels will you deny?

66 In them are two gushing springs.

67 So which of your Lord's marvels will you deny?

68 In them are fruits, and date-palms, and pomegranates.

69 So which of your Lord's marvels will you deny?

70 In them are good and beautiful ones.

71 So which of your Lord's marvels will you deny?

72 Companions, secluded in the tents.

73 So which of your Lord's marvels will you deny?

74 Whom no human has touched before, nor jinn.

75 So which of your Lord's marvels will you deny?

76 Reclining on green cushions, and exquisite carpets.

77 So which of your Lord's marvels will you deny?

78 Blessed be the name of your Lord, Full of Majesty and Splendor.

The Inevitable (al-Waqi'ah)

In the name of God, the Gracious, the Merciful.

1 When the inevitable occurs.

2 Of its occurrence, there is no denial.

3 Bringing low, raising high.

4 When the earth is shaken with a shock.

5 And the mountains are crushed and crumbled.

6 And they become scattered dust.

7 And you become three classes.

8 Those on the Right—what of those on the Right?

9 And those on the Left—what of those on the Left?

10 And the forerunners, the forerunners.

11 Those are the nearest.

12 In the Gardens of Bliss.

13 A throng from the ancients.

14 And a small band from the latecomers.

15 On luxurious furnishings.

16 Reclining on them, facing one another.

17 Serving them will be immortalized youth.

18 With cups, pitchers, and sparkling drinks.

19 Causing them neither headache, nor intoxication.

20 And fruits of their choice.

21 And meat of birds that they may desire.

22 And lovely companions.

23 The likenesses of treasured pearls.

24 As a reward for what they used to do.

25 Therein they will hear no nonsense, and no accusations.

26 But only the greeting: "Peace, peace."

27 And those on the Right—what of those on the Right?

28 In lush orchards.

29 And sweet-smelling plants.

30 And extended shade.

31 And outpouring water.

32 And abundant fruit.

33 Neither withheld, nor forbidden.

34 And uplifted mattresses.

35 We have created them of special creation.

36 And made them virgins.

37 Tender and un-aging.

38 For those on the Right.

39 A throng from the ancients.

40 And a throng from the latecomers.

41 And those on the Left—what of those on the Left?

42 Amid searing wind and boiling water.

43 And a shadow of thick smoke.

44 Neither cool, nor refreshing.

45 They had lived before that in luxury.

46 And they used to persist in immense wrongdoing.

47 And they used to say, "When we are dead and turned into dust and bones, are we to be resurrected?

48 And our ancient ancestors too?"

49 Say, "The first and the last.

50 Will be gathered for the appointment of a familiar Day."

51 Then you, you misguided, who deny the truth.

52 Will be eating from the Tree of Bitterness.

53 Will be filling your bellies with it.

54 Will be drinking on top of it boiling water.

55 Drinking like thirsty camels drink.

56 That is their hospitality on the Day of Retribution.

57 We created you—if only you would believe!

58 Have you seen what you ejaculate?

59 Is it you who create it, or are We the Creator?

60 We have decreed death among you, and We will not be outstripped.

61 In replacing you with your likes, and transforming you into what you do not know.

62 You have known the first formation; if only you would remember.

63 Have you seen what you cultivate?

64 Is it you who make it grow, or are We the Grower?

65 If We will, We can turn it into rubble; then you will lament.

66 "We are penalized.

67 No, we are being deprived."

68 Have you seen the water you drink?

69 Is it you who sent it down from the clouds, or are We the Sender?

70 If We will, We can make it salty. Will you not be thankful?

71 Have you seen the fire you kindle?

72 Is it you who produce its tree, or are We the Producer?

73 We have made it a reminder, and a comfort for the users.

74 So glorify the Name of your Great Lord.

75 I swear by the locations of the stars.

76 It is an oath, if you only knew, that is tremendous.

77 It is a noble Quran.

78 In a well-protected Book.

79 None can grasp it except the purified.

80 A revelation from the Lord of the Worlds.

81 Is it this discourse that you take so lightly?

82 And you make it your livelihood to deny it?

83 So when it has reached the throat.

84 As you are looking on.

85 We are nearer to it than you are, but you do not see.

86 If you are not held to account.

87 Then bring it back, if you are truthful.

88 But if he is one of those brought near.

89 Then happiness, and flowers, and Garden of Delights.

90 And if he is one of those on the Right.

91 Then, "Peace upon you," from those on the Right.

92 But if he is one of the deniers, the mistaken.

93 Then a welcome of Inferno.

94 And burning in Hell.

95 This is the certain truth.

96 So glorify the Name of your Lord, the Magnificent

Iron (al-Hadid')

In the name of God, the Gracious, the Merciful.

1 Glorifying God is everything in the heavens and the earth. He is the Almighty, the Wise.

2 To Him belongs the kingdom of the heavens and the earth. He gives life and causes death, and He has power over all things.

3 He is the First and the Last, and the Outer and the Inner, and He has knowledge of all things.

4 It is He who created the heavens and the earth in six days, then settled over the Throne. He knows what penetrates into the earth, and what comes out of it, and what descends from the sky, and what ascends to it. And He is with you wherever you may be. God is Seeing of everything you do.

5 To Him belongs the kingship of the heavens and the earth, and to God all matters are referred.

6 He merges the night into the day, and He merges the day into the night; and He knows what the hearts contains.

7 Believe in God and His Messenger, and spend from what He made you inherit. Those among you who believe and give will have a great reward.

8 What is the matter with you that you do not believe in God, when the Messenger calls you to believe in your Lord, and He has received a pledge from you, if you are believers?

9 It is He who sends down upon His servant clear revelations, to bring you out of darkness into the light. God is Gentle towards you, Most Compassionate.

10 And why is it that you do not spend in the cause of God, when to God belongs the inheritance of the heavens and the earth? Not equal among you are

those who contributed before the conquest, and fought. Those are higher in rank than those who contributed afterwards, and fought. But God promises both a good reward. God is Well Experienced in what you do.

11 Who is he who will lend God a loan of goodness, that He may double it for him, and will have a generous reward?

12 On the Day when you see the believing men and believing women—their light radiating ahead of them, and to their right: "Good news for you today: gardens beneath which rivers flow, dwelling therein forever. That is the great triumph."

13 On the Day when the hypocritical men and hypocritical women will say to those who believed, "Wait for us; let us absorb some of your light." It will be said, "Go back behind you, and seek light." A wall will be raised between them, in which is a door; within it is mercy, and outside it is agony.

14 They will call to them, "Were we not with you?" They will say, "Yes, but you cheated your souls, and waited, and doubted, and became deluded by wishful thinking, until the command of God arrived; and arrogance deceived you regarding God."

15 "Therefore, today no ransom will be accepted from you, nor from those who disbelieved. The Fire is your refuge. It is your companion—what an evil fate!"

16 Is it not time for those who believe to surrender their hearts to the remembrance of God, and to the truth that has come down, and not be like those who were given the Book previously, but time became prolonged for them, so their hearts hardened, and many of them are sinners?

17 Know that God revives the earth after its death. We thus explain the revelations for you, so that you may understand.

18 The charitable men and charitable women, who have loaned God a loan of righteousness—it will be multiplied for them, and for them is a generous reward.

19 Those who believe in God and His messengers—these are the sincere and the witnesses with their Lord; they will have their reward and their light. But as for those who disbelieve and deny Our revelations—these are the inmates of the Blaze.

20 Know that the worldly life is only play, and distraction, and glitter, and boasting among you, and rivalry in wealth and children. It is like a rainfall that produces plants, and delights the disbelievers. But then it withers, and you see it yellowing, and then it becomes debris. While in the Hereafter there is severe agony, and forgiveness from God, and acceptance. The life of this world is nothing but enjoyment of vanity.

21 Race towards forgiveness from your Lord; and a Garden as vast as the heavens and the earth, prepared for those who believe in God and His messengers. That is the grace of God; He bestows it on whomever He wills. God is the Possessor of Immense Grace.

22 No calamity occurs on earth, or in your souls, but it is in a Book, even before We make it happen. That is easy for God.

23 That you may not sorrow over what eludes you, nor exult over what He has given you. God does not love the proud snob.

24 Those who are stingy, and induce people to be stingy. Whoever turns away—God is the Independent, the Praiseworthy.

25 We sent Our messengers with the clear proofs, and We sent down with them the Book and the Balance, that humanity may uphold justice. And We sent down iron, in which is violent force, and benefits for humanity. That God may know who supports Him and His messengers invisibly. God is Strong and Powerful.

26 We sent Noah and Abraham, and established in their line Prophethood and the Scripture. Some of them are guided, but many of them are sinners.

27 Then We sent in their wake Our messengers, and followed up with Jesus son of Mary, and We gave him the Gospel, and instilled in the hearts of those who followed him compassion and mercy. But as for the monasticism which they invented—We did not ordain it for them—only to seek God's approval. But they did not observe it with its due observance. So We gave those of them who believed their reward, but many of them are sinful.

28 O you who believe! Fear God, and believe in His Messenger: He will give you a double portion of His mercy, and will give you a light by which you walk, and will forgive you. God is Forgiving and Merciful.

29 That the People of the Book may know that they have no power whatsoever over God's grace, and that all grace is in God's hand; He gives it to whomever He wills. God is Possessor of Great Grace.

Column (as-Saff)

In the name of God, the Gracious, the Merciful.

1 Everything in the heavens and the earth praises God. He is the Almighty, the Wise.

2 O you who believe! Why do you say what you do not do?

3 It is most hateful to God that you say what you do not do.

4 God loves those who fight in His cause, in ranks, as though they were a compact structure.

5 When Moses said to his people, "O my people, why do you hurt me, although you know that I am God's Messenger to you?" And when they swerved, God swerved their hearts. God does not guide the sinful people.

6 And when Jesus son of Mary said, "O Children of Israel, I am God's Messenger to you, confirming what preceded me of the Torah, and announcing good news of a messenger who will come after me, whose name is Ahmad." But when he showed them the miracles, they said, "This is obvious sorcery."

7 And who is a greater wrongdoer than he who attributes falsehoods to God, when he is being invited to Islam? God does not guide the wrongdoing people.

8 They want to extinguish God's Light with their mouths; but God will complete His Light, even though the disbelievers dislike it.

9 It is He who sent His Messenger with the guidance and the true religion, to make it prevail over all religions, even though the idolaters dislike it.

10 O you who believe! Shall I inform you of a trade that will save you from a painful torment?

11 That you believe in God and His Messenger, and strive in the cause of God with your possessions and yourselves. That is best for you, if you only knew.

12 He will forgive you your sins; and will admit you into gardens beneath which rivers flow, and into beautiful mansions in the Gardens of Eden. That is the supreme success.

13 And something else you love: support from God, and imminent victory. So give good news to the believers.

14 O you who believe! Be supporters of God, as Jesus son of Mary said to the disciples, "Who are my supporters towards God?" The disciples said, "We are God's supporters." So a group of the Children of Israel believed, while another

group disbelieved. We supported those who believed against their foe, so they became dominant.

Gathering (at-Taghabun)

In the name of God, the Gracious, the Merciful.

1 Everything in the heavens and the earth praises God. To Him belongs the Kingdom, and to Him all praise is due, and He is Able to do all things.

2 It is He who created you. Some of you are unbelievers, and some of you are believers. And God perceives what you do.

3 He created the heavens and the earth with truth, and He designed you, and designed you well, and to Him is the final return.

4 He knows everything in the heavens and the earth, and He knows what you conceal and what you reveal. And God knows what is within the hearts.

5 Has the news not reached you, of those who disbelieved before? They tasted the ill consequences of their conduct, and a painful torment awaits them.

6 That is because their messengers came to them with clear explanations, but they said, "Are human beings going to guide us?" So they disbelieved and turned away. But God is in no need. God is Independent and Praiseworthy.

7 Those who disbelieve claim that they will not be resurrected. Say, "Yes indeed, by my Lord, you will be resurrected; then you will be informed of everything you did; and that is easy for God."

8 So believe in God and His Messenger, and the Light which We sent down. God is Aware of everything you do.

9 The Day when He gathers you for the Day of Gathering—that is the Day of Mutual Exchange. Whoever believes in God and acts with integrity, He will remit his misdeeds, and will admit him into gardens beneath which rivers flow, to dwell therein forever. That is the supreme achievement.

10 But as for those who disbelieve and denounce Our revelations—these are the inmates of the Fire, dwelling therein forever; and what a miserable fate!

11 No disaster occurs except by God's leave. Whoever believes in God, He guides his heart. God is Aware of everything.

12 So obey God, and obey the Messenger. But if you turn away—it is only incumbent on Our Messenger to deliver the clear message.

13 God, there is no god but He; and in God let the believers put their trust.

14 O you who believe! Among your wives and your children are enemies to you, so beware of them. But if you pardon, and overlook, and forgive—God is Forgiver and Merciful.

15 Your possessions and your children are a test, but with God is a splendid reward.

16 So be conscious of God as much as you can, and listen, and obey, and give for your own good. He who is protected from his stinginess—these are the prosperous.

17 If you lend God a good loan, He will multiply it for you, and will forgive you. God is Appreciative and Forbearing.

18 The Knower of the Unseen and the Seen, the Almighty, the Wise.

The Enwrapped (al-Muzzammil)

In the name of God, the Gracious, the Merciful.

1 O you Enwrapped one.

2 Stay up during the night, except a little.

3 For half of it, or reduce it a little.

4 Or add to it; and chant the Quran rhythmically.

5 We are about to give you a heavy message.

6 The vigil of night is more effective, and better suited for recitation.

7 In the daytime, you have lengthy work to do.

8 So remember the Name of your Lord, and devote yourself to Him wholeheartedly.

9 Lord of the East and the West. There is no god but He, so take Him as a Trustee.

10 And endure patiently what they say, and withdraw from them politely.

11 And leave Me to those who deny the truth, those of luxury, and give them a brief respite.

12 With Us are shackles, and a Fierce Fire.

13 And food that chokes, and a painful punishment.

14 On the Day when the earth and the mountains tremble, and the mountains become heaps of sand.

15 We have sent to you a messenger, a witness over you, as We sent to Pharaoh a messenger.

16 But Pharaoh defied the Messenger, so We seized him with a terrible seizing.

17 So how will you, if you persist in unbelief, save yourself from a Day which will turn the children gray-haired?

18 The heaven will shatter thereby. His promise is always fulfilled.

19 This is a reminder. So whoever wills, let him take a path to his Lord.

20 Your Lord knows that you stay up nearly two-thirds of the night, or half of it, or one-third of it, along with a group of those with you. God designed the night and the day. He knows that you are unable to sustain it, so He has pardoned you. So read of the Quran what is possible for you. He knows that some of you may be ill; and others travelling through the land, seeking God's bounty; and others fighting in God's cause. So read of it what is possible for you, and observe the prayers, and give regular charity, and lend God a generous loan. Whatever good you advance for yourselves, you will find it with God, better and generously rewarded. And seek God's forgiveness, for God is Forgiving and Merciful.

The Enrobed (al-Muddathir)

In the name of God, the Gracious, the Merciful.

1 O you Enrobed one.

2 Arise and warn.

3 And magnify your Lord.

4 And purify your clothes.

5 And abandon abominations.

6 And show no favor seeking gain.

7 And be constant for your Lord.

8 When the Trumpet is blown.

9 That Day will be a difficult day.

10 For the disbelievers—not easy.

11 Leave Me to him whom I created alone.

12 And gave him vast wealth.

13 And children as witnesses.

14 And smoothed things for him.

15 Then he wants Me to add yet more!

16 By no means! He was stubborn towards Our revelations.

17 I will exhaust him increasingly.

18 He thought and analyzed.

19 May he perish, how he analyzed.

20 Again: may he perish, how he analyzed.

21 Then he looked.

22 Then he frowned and whined.

23 Then he turned back and was proud.

24 And said, "This is nothing but magic from the past.

25 This is nothing but the word of a mortal."

26 I will roast him in Saqar.

27 But what will explain to you what Saqar is?

28 It neither leaves, nor spares.

29 It scorches the flesh.

30 Over it are Nineteen.

31 We have appointed only angels to be wardens of the Fire, and caused their number to be a stumbling block for those who disbelieve; so that those given the Scripture may attain certainty; and those who believe may increase in faith; and those given the Scripture and the believers may not doubt; and those in whose hearts is sickness and the unbelievers may say, "What did God intend by this parable?" Thus God leads astray whom He wills, and guides whom He wills. None knows the soldiers of your Lord except He. This is nothing but a reminder for the mortals.

32 Nay! By the moon.

33 And the night as it retreats.

34 And the morning as it lights up.

35 It is one of the greatest.

36 A warning to the mortals.

37 To whomever among you wishes to advance, or regress.

38 Every soul is hostage to what it has earned.

39 Except for those on the Right.

40 In Gardens, inquiring.

41 About the guilty.

42 "What drove you into Saqar?"

43 They will say, "We were not of those who prayed.

44 Nor did we feed the destitute.

45 And we used to indulge with those who indulge.

46 And we used to deny the Day of Judgment.

47 Until the Inevitable came upon us."

48 But the intercession of intercessors will not help them.

49 Why are they turning away from the Reminder?

50 As though they were panicked donkeys.

51 Fleeing from a lion?

52 Yet every one of them desires to be given scrolls unrolled.

53 No indeed! But they do not fear the Hereafter.

54 Nevertheless, it is a reminder.

55 So whoever wills, shall remember it.

56 But they will not remember, unless God wills. He is the Source of Righteousness, and the Source of Forgiveness.

Resurrection (al-Qiyamah)

In the name of God, the Gracious, the Merciful.

1 I swear by the Day of Resurrection.

2 And I swear by the blaming soul.

3 Does man think that We will not reassemble his bones?

4 Yes indeed; We are Able to reconstruct his fingertips.

5 But man wants to deny what is ahead of him.

6 He asks, "When is the Day of Resurrection?"

7 When vision is dazzled.

8 And the moon is eclipsed.

9 And the sun and the moon are joined together.

10 On that Day, man will say, "Where is the escape?"

11 No indeed! There is no refuge.

12 To your Lord on that Day is the settlement.

13 On that Day man will be informed of everything he put forward, and everything he left behind.

14 And man will be evidence against himself.

15 Even as he presents his excuses.

16 Do not wag your tongue with it, to hurry on with it.

17 Upon Us is its collection and its recitation.

18 Then, when We have recited it, follow its recitation.

19 Then upon Us is its explanation.

20 Alas, you love the fleeting life.

21 And you disregard the Hereafter.

22 Faces on that Day will be radiant.

23 Looking towards their Lord.

24 And faces on that Day will be gloomy.

25 Realizing that a back-breaker has befallen them.

26 Indeed, when it has reached the breast-bones.

27 And it is said, "Who is the healer?"

28 And He realizes that it is the parting.

29 And leg is entwined with leg.

30 To your Lord on that Day is the drive.

31 He neither believed nor prayed.

32 But he denied and turned away.

33 Then he went to his family, full of pride.

34 Woe to you; and woe.

35 Then again: Woe to you; and woe.

36 Does man think that he will be left without purpose?

37 Was he not a drop of ejaculated semen?

38 Then he became a clot. And He created and proportioned?

39 And made of him the two sexes, the male and the female?

40 Is He not Able to revive the dead?

The Event (an-Naba')

In the name of God, the Gracious, the Merciful.

1 What are they asking one another about?

2 About the Great Event.

3 About which they disagree.

4 Surely, they will find out.

5 Most certainly, they will find out.

6 Did We not make the earth a cradle?

7 And the mountains pegs?

8 And created you in pairs?

9 And made your sleep for rest?

10 And made the night a cover?

11 And made the day for livelihood?

12 And built above you seven strong ones?

13 And placed a blazing lamp?

14 And brought down from the clouds pouring water?

15 To produce with it grains and vegetation?

16 And luxuriant gardens?

17 The Day of Sorting has been appointed.

18 The Day when the Trumpet is blown, and you will come in droves.

19 And the sky is opened up, and becomes gateways.

20 And the mountains are set in motion, and become a mirage.

21 Hell is lying in ambush.

22 For the oppressors, a destination.

23 Where they will remain for eons.

24 They will taste therein neither coolness, nor drink.

25 Except boiling water, and freezing hail.

26 A fitting requital.

27 For they were not anticipating any reckoning.

28 And they denied Our signs utterly.

29 But We have enumerated everything in writing.

30 So taste! We will increase you only in suffering.

31 But for the righteous there is triumph.

32 Gardens and vineyards.

33 And splendid spouses, well matched.

34 And delicious drinks.

35 They will hear therein neither gossip, nor lies.

36 A reward from your Lord, a fitting gift.

37 Lord of the heavens and the earth, and everything between them—The Most Merciful—none can argue with Him.

38 On the Day when the Spirit and the angels stand in row. They will not speak, unless it be one permitted by the Most Merciful, and he will say what is right.

39 That is the Day of Reality. So whoever wills, let him take a way back to his Lord.

40 We have warned you of a near punishment—the Day when a person will observe what his hands have produced, and the faithless will say, "O, I wish I were dust."

The Rolling (at-Takwir)

In the name of God, the Gracious, the Merciful.

1 When the sun is rolled up.

2 When the stars are dimmed.

3 When the mountains are set in motion.

4 When the relationships are suspended.

5 When the beasts are gathered.

6 When the oceans are set aflame.

7 When the souls are paired.

8 When the girl, buried alive, is asked:

9 For what crime was she killed?

10 When the records are made public.

11 When the sky is peeled away.

12 When the Fire is set ablaze.

13 When Paradise is brought near.

14 Each soul will know what it has readied.

15 I swear by the galaxies.

16 Precisely running their courses.

17 And by the night as it recedes.

18 And by the morn as it breathes.

19 This is the speech of a noble messenger.

20 Endowed with power, eminent with the Lord of the Throne.

21 Obeyed and honest.

22 Your friend is not possessed.

23 He saw him on the luminous horizon.

24 And He does not withhold knowledge of the Unseen.

25 And it is not the word of an accursed devil.

26 So where are you heading?

27 It is only a Reminder to all mankind.

28 To whoever of you wills to go straight.

29 But you cannot will, unless God wills—The Lord of the Worlds.

The Shattering (al-Infitar)

In the name of God, the Gracious, the Merciful.

1 When the sky breaks apart.

2 When the planets are scattered.

3 When the oceans are exploded.

4 When the tombs are strewn around.

5 Each soul will know what it has advanced, and what it has deferred.

6 O man! What deluded you concerning your Lord, the Most Generous?

7 He Who created you, and formed you, and proportioned you?

8 In whatever shape He willed, He assembled you.

9 But you reject the religion.

10 Though over you are watchers.

11 Honest recorders.

12 They know everything you do.

13 The virtuous will be in bliss.

14 While the wicked will be in Hell.

15 They will enter it on the Day of Justice.

16 And they will not be absent from it.

17 But what will convey to you what the Day of Justice is?

18 Then again, what will convey to you what the Day of Justice is?

19 The Day when no soul will avail another soul anything; and the decision on that Day is God's.

The Defrauders (al-Mutaffifin)

In the name of God, the Gracious, the Merciful.

1 Woe to the defrauders.

2 Those who, when they take a measure from people, they take in full.

3 But when they measure or weigh to others, they cheat.

4 Do these not know that they will be resurrected?

5 For a Great Day?

6 The Day when mankind will stand before the Lord of the Worlds?

7 Not at all. The record of the wicked is in Sijjeen.

8 But how can you know what Sijjeen is?

9 A numerical book.

10 Woe on that Day to the deniers.

11 Those who deny the Day of Reckoning.

12 But none denies it except the sinful aggressor.

13 When Our revelations are recited to him, he says, "Legends of the ancients."

14 Not at all. Their hearts have become corroded by what they used to earn.

15 Not at all. On that Day, they will be screened from their Lord.

16 Then they will roast in Hell.

17 Then it will be said, "This is what you used to deny."

18 No indeed; the record of the righteous is in Elliyyeen.

19 But how can you know what Elliyyoon is?

20 A numerical book.

21 Witnessed by those brought near.

22 Indeed, the righteous will be amid bliss.

23 On thrones, looking on.

24 You will recognize on their faces the radiance of bliss.

25 They will be given to drink a sealed wine.

26 Whose seal is musk—this is what competitors should compete for.

27 Its mixture is of Tasneem.

28 A spring from which those brought near drink.

29 Those who committed crimes used to laugh at those who believed.

30 And when they passed by them, they would wink at one another.

31 And when they went back to their families, they would go back exulting.

32 And if they saw them, they would say, "These people are lost."

33 Yet they were not sent as guardians over them.

34 But on that Day, those who believed will laugh at the unbelievers.

35 On luxurious furnishings, looking on.

36 Have the unbelievers been repaid for what they used to do?

The Rupture (al-Inshiqaq)

In the name of God, the Gracious, the Merciful.

1 When the sky is ruptured.

2 And hearkens to its Lord, as it must.

3 And when the earth is leveled out.

4 And casts out what is in it, and becomes empty.

5 And hearkens to its Lord, as it must.

6 O man! You are laboring towards your Lord, and you will meet Him.

7 As for him who is given his book in his right hand.

8 He will have an easy settlement.

9 And will return to his family delighted.

10 But as for him who is given his book behind his back.

11 He will call for death.

12 And will enter the Blaze.

13 He used to be happy among his family.

14 He thought he would never return.

15 In fact, his Lord was watching him.

16 I swear by the twilight.

17 And by the night, and what it covers.

18 And by the moon, as it grows full.

19 You will mount stage by stage.

20 What is the matter with them that they do not believe?

21 And when the Quran is read to them, they do not bow down?

22 In fact, those who disbelieve are in denial.

23 But God knows what they hide inside.

24 So inform them of a painful punishment.

25 Except those who believe and do good deeds; they will have an undiminished reward.

The Constellations (al-Buruj)

In the name of God, the Gracious, the Merciful.

1 By the sky with the constellations.

2 And by the Promised Day.

3 And by the witness and the witnessed.

4 Destroyed were the People of the Trench.

5 The fire supplied with fuel.

6 While they sat around it.

7 And were witnessing what they did to the believers.

8 They begrudged them only because they believed in God the Almighty, the Praiseworthy.

9 To Whom belongs the sovereignty of the heavens and the earth. God is witness over everything.

10 Those who tempt the believers, men and women, then do not repent; for them is the punishment of Hell; for them is the punishment of Burning.

11 Those who believe and do righteous deeds will have Gardens beneath which rivers flow. That is the great triumph.

12 The onslaught of your Lord is severe.

13 It is He who begins and repeats.

14 And He is the Forgiving, the Loving.

15 Possessor of the Glorious Throne.

16 Doer of whatever He wills.

17 Has there come to you the story of the legions?

18 Of Pharaoh and Thamood?

19 In fact, those who disbelieve are in denial.

20 And God encloses them from beyond.

21 In fact, it is a Glorious Quran.

22 In a Preserved Tablet.

The Most High (al-A'la)

In the name of God, the Gracious, the Merciful.

1 Praise the Name of your Lord, the Most High.

2 He who creates and regulates.

3 He who measures and guides.

4 He who produces the pasture.

5 And then turns it into light debris.

6 We will make you read, so do not forget.

7 Except what God wills. He knows what is declared, and what is hidden.

8 We will ease you into the Easy Way.

9 So remind, if reminding helps.

10 The reverent will remember.

11 But the wretched will avoid it.

12 He who will enter the Gigantic Fire.

13 Where he will neither die, nor live.

14 Successful is he who purifies himself.

15 And mentions the name of his Lord, and prays.

16 But you prefer the present life.

17 Though the Hereafter is better, and more lasting.

18 This is in the former scriptures.

19 The Scriptures of Abraham and Moses.

The Overwhelming (al-Ghashiyah)

In the name of God, the Gracious, the Merciful.

1 Has there come to you the news of the overwhelming?

2 Faces on that Day will be shamed.

3 Laboring and exhausted.

4 Roasting in a scorching Fire.

5 Given to drink from a flaming spring.

6 They will have no food except thorns.

7 That neither nourishes, nor satisfies hunger.

8 Faces on that Day will be joyful.

9 Satisfied with their endeavor.

10 In a lofty Garden.

11 In it you will hear no nonsense.

12 In it is a flowing spring.

13 In it are raised beds.

14 And cups set in place.

15 And cushions set in rows.

16 And carpets spread around.

17 Do they not look at the camels—how they are created?

18 And at the sky—how it is raised?

19 And at the mountains—how they are installed?

20 And at the earth—how it is spread out?

21 So remind. You are only a reminder.

22 You have no control over them.

23 But whoever turns away and disbelieves.

24 God will punish him with the greatest punishment.

25 To Us is their return.

26 Then upon Us rests their reckoning.

The Dawn (al-Fajr)

In the name of God, the Gracious, the Merciful.

1 By the daybreak.

2 And ten nights.

3 And the even and the odd.

4 And the night as it recedes.

5 Is there in this an oath for a rational person?

6 Have you not seen how your Lord dealt with Aad?

7 Erum of the pillars.

8 The like of which was never created in the land.

9 And Thamood—those who carved the rocks in the valley.

10 And Pharaoh of the Stakes.

11 Those who committed excesses in the lands.

12 And spread much corruption therein.

13 So your Lord poured down upon them a scourge of punishment.

14 Your Lord is on the lookout.

15 As for man, whenever his Lord tests him, and honors him, and prospers him, he says, "My Lord has honored me."

16 But whenever He tests him, and restricts his livelihood for him, he says, "My Lord has insulted me."

17 Not at all. But you do not honor the orphan.

18 And you do not urge the feeding of the poor.

19 And you devour inheritance with all greed.

20 And you love wealth with immense love.

21 No—when the earth is leveled, pounded, and crushed.

22 And your Lord comes, with the angels, row after row.

23 And on that Day, Hell is brought forward. On that Day, man will remember, but how will remembrance avail him?

24 He will say, "If only I had forwarded for my life."

25 On that Day, none will punish as He punishes.

26 And none will shackle as He shackles.

27 But as for you, O tranquil soul.

28 Return to your Lord, pleased and accepted.

29 Enter among My servants.

30 Enter My Paradise.

The Land (al-Balad)

In the name of God, the Gracious, the Merciful.

1 I swear by this land.

2 And you are a resident of this land.

3 And by a father and what he fathered.

4 We created man in distress.

5 Does he think that no one has power over him?

6 He says, "I have used up so much money."

7 Does he think that no one sees him?

8 Did We not give him two eyes?

9 And a tongue, and two lips?

10 And We showed him the two ways?

11 But he did not brave the ascent.

12 And what will explain to you what the ascent is?

13 The freeing of a slave.

14 Or the feeding on a day of hunger.

15 An orphan near of kin.

16 Or a destitute in the dust.

17 Then he becomes of those who believe, and advise one another to patience, and advise one another to kindness.

18 These are the people of happiness.

19 But as for those who defy Our revelations—these are the people of misery.

20 Upon them is a padlocked Fire.

The Night (al-Layl)

In the name of God, the Gracious, the Merciful.

1 By the night as it covers.

2 And the day as it reveals.

3 And He who created the male and the female.

4 Your endeavors are indeed diverse.

5 As for him who gives and is righteous.

6 And confirms goodness.

7 We will ease his way towards ease.

8 But as for him who is stingy and complacent.

9 And denies goodness.

10 We will ease his way towards difficulty.

11 And his money will not avail him when he plummets.

12 It is upon Us to guide.

13 And to Us belong the Last and the First.

14 I have warned you of a Fierce Blaze.

15 None will burn in it except the very wicked.

16 He who denies and turns away.

17 But the devout will avoid it.

18 He who gives his money to become pure.

19 Seeking no favor in return.

20 Only seeking the acceptance of his Lord, the Most High.

21 And he will be satisfied.

Morning Light (adh-Duha)

In the name of God, the Gracious, the Merciful.

1 By the morning light.

2 And the night as it settles.

3 Your Lord did not abandon you, nor did He forget.

4 The Hereafter is better for you than the First.

5 And your Lord will give you, and you will be satisfied.

6 Did He not find you orphaned, and sheltered you?

7 And found you wandering, and guided you?

8 And found you in need, and enriched you?

9 Therefore, do not mistreat the orphan.

10 Nor rebuff the seeker.

11 But proclaim the blessings of your Lord.

The Soothing (ash-Sharh)

In the name of God, the Gracious, the Merciful.

1 Did We not soothe your heart?

2 And lift from you your burden.

3 Which weighed down your back?

4 And raised for you your reputation?

5 With hardship comes ease.

6 With hardship comes ease.

7 When your work is done, turn to devotion.

8 And to your Lord turn for everything.

The Fig (at-Tin)

In the name of God, the Gracious, the Merciful.

1 By the fig and the olive.

2 And Mount Sinai.

3 And this safe land.

4 We created man in the best design.

5 Then reduced him to the lowest of the low.

6 Except those who believe and do righteous deeds; for them is a reward without end.

7 So why do you still reject the religion?

8 Is God not the Wisest of the wise?

Decree (al-Qadr)

In the name of God, the Gracious, the Merciful.

1 We sent it down on the Night of Decree.

2 But what will convey to you what the Night of Decree is?

3 The Night of Decree is better than a thousand months.

4 In it descend the angels and the Spirit, by the leave of their Lord, with every command.

5 Peace it is; until the rise of dawn.

The Quake (az-Zalzalah)

In the name of God, the Gracious, the Merciful.

1 When the earth is shaken with its quake.

2 And the earth brings out its loads.

3 And man says, "What is the matter with it?"

4 On that Day, it will tell its tales.

5 For your Lord will have inspired it.

6 On that Day, the people will emerge in droves, to be shown their works.

7 Whoever has done an atom's weight of good will see it.

8 And whoever has done an atom's weight of evil will see it.

Time (al-'Asr)

In the name of God, the Gracious, the Merciful.

1 By Time.

2 The human being is in loss.

3 Except those who believe, and do good works, and encourage truth, and recommend patience.

The Backbiter (al-Humazah)

In the name of God, the Gracious, the Merciful.

1 Woe to every slanderer backbiter.

2 Who gathers wealth and counts it over.

3 Thinking that his wealth has made him immortal.

4 By no means. He will be thrown into the Crusher.

5 And what will make you realize what the Crusher is?

6 God's kindled Fire.

7 That laps to the hearts.

8 It closes in on them.

9 In extended columns.

The Disbelievers (al-Kafirun)

In the name of God, the Gracious, the Merciful.

1 Say, "O disbelievers.

2 I do not worship what you worship.

3 Nor do you worship what I worship.

4 Nor do I serve what you serve.

5 Nor do you serve what I serve.

6 You have your way, and I have my way."

Monotheism (al-Ikhlas)

In the name of God, the Gracious, the Merciful.

1 Say, "He is God, the One.

2 God, the Absolute.

3 He begets not, nor was He begotten.

4 And there is nothing comparable to Him."

www.ingramcontent.com/pod-product-compliance
Lightning Source LLC
Chambersburg PA
CBHW071503040426
42444CB00008B/1468